The New Mavericks

Gen Z's Guide to Redefining the Workplace

Nicky Foster

Ainslie Street
Publishing

ISBN: 979-8-9887779-5-3 (Paperback)

ISBN: 979-8-9887779-6-0 (Hardback)

Ainslie Street Publishing

Published in Brooklyn, NY

Ainslie Street Publishing

Ainslie Street Publishing is an independent publishing house based in Brooklyn, NY.

As a token of our gratitude for your purchase, we would like to send you a free book. Use your phone's camera app and scan the QR code below to receive it.

CONTENTS

INTRODUCTION

Generation Z, there is no doubt that you have it rough compared to previous generations entering the workforce. You feel unheard by other generations in the workplace, even when you know your taboo ideas and tech-savvy approach will launch success. You prioritize life over work, but at the same time, you want to make a difference and feel that your contributions matter.

The truth is, you're not alone. The workforce has changed dramatically over the last decade, and the pandemic ushered in a new workplace environment founded on the need for diversity, cross-generational communication, mental health awareness, and remote work.

As pointed out by Jack Kelly in Forbes, the pandemic changed the workforce in irreversible ways. Coding and communication skills are in high demand, while grit, resilience, and adapting to change are considered mandatory traits (Kelly, 2020). That describes you, Gen Zer.

A 2022 Gallup study also found that 61% of workers want a better work/life balance, not just Generation Z. Flexibility and paid time off to improve mental health are becoming highly desirable when seeking employment, but Zoomers are the ones driving employers to make the change due to their vocal objections to putting work first (Moss, 2022).

Furthermore, while some employers are slow to get on the bandwagon, a 2021 Mercer study found that 76% of employers surveyed said addressing mental and emotional health would be a priority in the next three to five years. Change is happening, but it is slow.

What your generation, and others, have failed to recognize is that you are uniquely able to thrive in this new global workplace. You are young, but you are also the most tech-savvy. You can adapt to change because it is all you have ever known. Through a relationship with an effective mentor, you can get your ideas heard and make a significant contribution without the need to move quickly up the crowded ladder.

This book aims to show you how to take advantage of your skills, talents, and the real and perceived characteristics of your generation to further change and enhance the current employment landscape. We will also discuss how to avoid the pitfalls and overcome the obstacles facing Generation Z in the workplace.

While many of the obstacles and challenges you will face as you enter the workforce have been hurdled by the generations before you, they are more difficult to overcome in some ways. Being heard by others in the workplace can be a big challenge when the number of seniors in the workforce is expected to grow by 96.5% between 2021 and 2030 (U.S. Bureau of Labor Statistics, 2021). Communication skills are key in facing this challenge.

At the same time, participation in the labor force of those aged 16 to 24 is expected to shrink by 7.5% in the same time frame. This reflects the fact that as of July 2023, the labor force participation rate is just 62.6%, having been level for the previous three months (U.S. Bureau of Labor Statistics, n.d.). The biggest reason for this is that more and more people, particularly young people, are seeking out multiple streams of income that have nothing to do with regular employment.

This is a double-edged sword. While there are many other opportunities for Gen Zers, the fact that the generation as a whole has opted to seek out alternative means of income also gives more traditional employers the impression that your generation simply isn't committed to a career.

What they don't understand is that the innovation and drive required to earn from multiple income streams could greatly benefit their company.

Generation Z has another obstacle – a high barrier to entry to even entry-level jobs. These are made even more trying by the fact that internships were scarce during the pandemic. Never fear, we'll show you how to overcome these obstacles in your job search and interviews in the coming pages.

But, there are also obstacles that other generations faced that you won't. For example, job hopping is no longer the taboo deal breaker for employers that it once was. Careers are expected to be diverse, encompassing a variety of companies and positions.

In the end, your generation has a unique opportunity to overcome these challenges and change the workplace in the process. Change is happening all around us at an incredible rate, and it will take the innovation and determination of Generation Z to make companies successful.

So, without further ado, let's dig in and show you how to take advantage of your unique position and make the most of it in your career.

PART 1: DEFINING FACTORS

Some things just need to be said about Generation Z. You know your characteristics, but do you know how to leverage them in your career and in the workplace? We're going to show you exactly how to do that in the coming chapters, but we must first discuss these defining factors in detail.

Why is this important?

The characteristics of Generation Z as a whole are important because they not only define who you are and what you can accomplish, but they also define how employers, managers, and coworkers see you.

Here we will discuss the opportunities and pitfalls that you must watch out for as you enter the workforce.

WHO YOU ARE MATTERS

L ET'S BEGIN BY DEFINING, "Who is Generation Z?" According to Pew Research, Generation Z encompasses all born between 1997 and 2012 (Dimock, 2019). The youngest Zoomers at the time of this writing are just 11 years old, but the upper end of the spectrum includes adults who are just entering the workforce or graduating college. Those born in 1996 or earlier in the 90s may also identify with some of the material within these pages.

Defining generations is arbitrary but important, and this definition of Generation Z is used by businesses and organizations across the country and around the globe. Having generational divisions allows researchers to determine common traits and trends among different demographics. While you may not identify with all of those traits or follow all of the trends, employers are going to lump you into this category in any case.

So let's dive into how Generation Z has been defined.

You Have Always Had Technology at Your Fingertips

Generation Z are considered "digital natives." According to Pew Research, who first set the boundaries of Gen Z, several characteristics are important considerations for your generation. The biggest of these is that you have never lived without technology at your fingertips.

Whereas Millennials adapted to an internet and social media-connected world, Generation Z has always had these tools at their fingertips. The first iPhone was released in 2007 when the oldest of Gen Z was just 10 years old. You don't need to be told this. Chances are you barely remember not having a tablet or mobile phone available whenever you wanted or needed it.

And, just as Millennials dominated computer industries while Generation X had to adapt, Generation Z has a leg up on the rest of the world when it comes to mobile technology and social media. You have an understanding and ease of use with this technology that other generations lack. You have also lived in a constant state of technological change.

This is a huge asset in the workplace. While some older generations may look down on Gen Zers for their constant use of mobile devices, the truth is that Generation Z has the best understanding of how to leverage these technologies to the benefit of older companies. A balance must be struck between making this advantage clear to employers while respecting the boundaries of personal technology use in the workplace.

You Have Always Lived In An Uncertain Economy

Another characteristic of Generation Z that affects your opportunities and challenges in the workplace is the economy. Millennials had to adjust to a recession, while Generation Z has never known economic security. Before the pandemic, the last major shift in the economy was the onset of the Great Recession in 2007, which didn't truly peak in recovery until February 2020 – just as the pandemic sent us into another Recession (*Chart Book: Tracking the Post-Great Recession Economy, 2022*). The end result is that you likely have never known economic or job security.

The economy has a large role to play in the employment of Generation Z, even when looking outside actual employment trends. The housing crisis has left many young people such as yourself without stable housing or being forced to continue living with family into adulthood. Housing situations and economic status impact mental health and an individual's ability to maintain stable employment.

You have Never Had Job Security

Perhaps the most challenging aspect of Generation Z is that you have never experienced job security. We live in an uncertain employment market, one where some industries are rife with competition while others are experiencing labor shortages. Unfortunately, the fields in which there are labor shortages are not the most common for Generation Z, at least not now.

It is far more likely that you have found yourself with a degree or in a trade for which there is steep competition. With higher barriers to employment, such as the need for internships for even entry-level positions, it is even harder to find steady work. Meanwhile, companies are falling short in many industries, closing their doors or cutting labor costs – and the positions that incur them.

This has some advantages and disadvantages for you, Gen Zer. It means that job hopping is no longer the taboo it once was. It is now considered normal for someone to change jobs within a year or two. This is really a new phenomenon since the pandemic and one that you should take advantage of.

In truth, the working world, and indeed the world in general, has never felt safe to most of Generation Z. This uncertainty and the desire to end it is one of the things that makes you so very special.

You Are More Accepting

Generation Z is the most accepting of all generations. You believe that everyone is equal and deserves the same opportunities. You expect employers to treat everyone the same. You don't tolerate unfair treatment of an employee because they are a woman, transgender, or otherwise diverse.

In fact, Gen Z is the most diverse generation to date. Nearly half of your generation are of mixed race, and 1 in 5 Zoomers identify as part of the LGBTQ+ community (Jones, 2022). Far more Gen Zers know someone who is transgender than any other generation. Gender norms don't make sense to you, and you fight them at every turn.

While the range of economic and political views of Generation Z are as varied as other generations, most of your generation believes that being socially liberal should be a given. And you are ready to do what needs to be done to make that a reality.

This drive and determination can easily be put to good use to create a more diverse and inclusive work environment.

You Are Health-Conscious

Generation Z is the most health-conscious generation to date. You are less likely to be a smoker, and more likely to eat a healthy diet. You are also more aware of mental health and wellness than previous generations, and you desire an employer that will prioritize your well-being over their profits.

This is not an easy thing to find, but it is becoming more common. Some larger employers offer paid time off that can be used as "mental health days," a new type of sick day. These "mental health days" are a great example of how Generation Z is making a difference in today's post-pandemic workplace.

You are Entrepreneurial

Generation Z is one of the most entrepreneurial generations, second only to Millenials, and perhaps only because much of Generation Z is still too young to enter the business world. That entrepreneurial spirit is a huge asset to employers, if they are only willing to see it.

Many employers see Generation Z as lazy because many of them didn't hold jobs in high school or through college, and many put off getting a driver's license. However, most Gen Zers eschewed traditional paycheck jobs to do product placements, run a side hustle, or sell a product or service that they themselves developed (Witte, 2022).

The easiest way to benefit from traditional employment is to find a company that understands the innovation and entrepreneurial drive of Generation Z and is willing to embrace it – and pay for your contributions.

You Are Interconnected Online and Off

Generation Z is the most connected generation to date, and not just online and through social media. While Gen Zers don't usually demand the validation expected by Millennials, they do expect transparency and open communication among their peers and with management. This is a foreign concept to most companies, who have traditionally given only instructions and feedback on an employee's individual contributions rather than their role in the company as a whole.

However, that doesn't mean you want all of this communication to be digital. A study conducted by Stanford University found that Generation Z actually prefers in-person communication over digital, even though they consider their mobile device to be an extension of themselves (Witte, 2022).

You Rely on Public Transportation

One of the reasons that Generation Z has been viewed as lazy by other generations is their failure to get a driver's license. Many employers require that a candidate have reliable transportation to and from work to be hired. When they ask about transportation in the interview, many employers are turned off by the fact that Gen Zers utilize Uber, Lyft, the bus, bikes, and other eco-friendly modes of transportation.

This is clearly seen by statistics reported by the Washington Post. In 1997, 43% of 16-year-olds and 62 percent of 17-year-olds had their driver's licenses. However, in 2020 just 25% of 16-year-olds and 45% of 17-year-olds had their license. In addition, many older Gen Zers between 20 and 25 don't drive, and only 80% of them have a driver's license.

So if you don't have a license or prefer eco-friendly and public transportation, you're not alone.

You Prioritize Life/Work Balance

Previous generations have not prioritized a life/work balance. Rather, they have let work take priority, even when it was detrimental to relationships and their mental health. However, Forbes reports that 38% of Generation Z report that achieving an optimal and healthy work/life balance, and prioritizing quality of life over their job is a high priority (Stahl, 2019).

You aren't alone in this. Millennials are also beginning to have a different work/life balance than their parents. Still, Gen Z is even more adamant that their work life should not interfere with their social life. This can be both a blessing and a curse because it is also important that you not allow your personal life to enter or inhibit your professional one.

You Aren't Afraid of Failure

The same Forbes article mentioned above also states that 80% of Gen Zers surveyed by human resources giant EY embrace failure as a way to succeed on future projects. As mentioned above, they expect measurable feedback that they can use to improve themselves and their work in the future.

Employers have yet to embrace this fact. Many employers still see failure as just – well, failure. However, often it is failure that leads to innovation and the overcoming of obstacles. The trick is to make employers see this for the betterment of their company and employees.

Now that we've taken a look at the traits that make up your generation, let's take a closer look at how they will affect your time in the workforce.

2

Gen Z's Magic

I N SOME WAYS, YOU are more prepared and capable of thriving in today's workforce than previous generations. It is important to understand how the magic of your generation can be applied successfully to today's workplace. Every job seeker of any age should have a realistic view of their strengths and weaknesses. Understanding these concepts will allow you to write better resumes, craft compelling cover letters, and make a lasting impression in job interviews.

Employers are starting to appreciate and value the magic that Gen Z brings to the conference table. According to the latest report from iCIMS, 53% of human resource departments are increasing their number of Gen Z hires in 2023 (*iCIMS Class of 2023 Report*, 2023).

This clearly shows that employers are starting to grasp that Generation Z has a lot to offer. Furthermore, employers are looking at the skills and capabilities of Gen Z candidates over academics. According to the National Association of Colleges and Employers (NACE), just 37% of employers are using GPA as an initial screening criteria, down 36.3% from 2019 (Gray, 2023).

Instead, NACE reports that employers are looking for specific skills and abilities, including problem-solving, the ability to work in a team, a strong work ethic, analytical and quantitative skills, communication skills, and technical skills. Most of these traits are naturally found in Generation Z candidates and correspond to the traits discussed in Chapter

One, although there are some pitfalls involved that we will discuss in the next chapter.

Let's look at how some of these desired capabilities are met by Gen Z's magic.

Problem Solving Skills

There are several traits of Gen Z that make you a better problem solver than an older employee. The primary methods of problem-solving are the use of algorithms, trial and error, and insights. With Gen Z's magic, these methods become much more effective.

It is well understood that, unlike Generation X and Millennials who feel overwhelmed and helpless to solve economic and environmental problems, your generation is ready to tackle those problems head-on. This forward-thinking is of great asset to employers.

To start, it is much easier to solve problems through trial and error when you aren't afraid of failure. Trial and error, either in reality or through the use of models, is the best way to know if you have found a viable solution to the problem at hand. Your ability to use technology to your advantage helps in this as well.

Generation Z is also the most embracing of AI technology such as ChatGPT. Such tools are vital in solving problems in the average workplace, but their effective use in problem-solving also requires analytical and critical research skills which Gen Zers have been drilled by their English Language Arts teachers since middle school.

The Ability to Work in a Team

The interconnectedness of your generation makes you better able to collaborate across departments and organizations to work as a team toward a common goal. Your ability and willingness to communicate through a variety of digital means or in person allows you to collaborate more effectively with others across generational gaps.

Even more important than this is your *desire* to work in a team and be part of something bigger than yourself. Your generation is hyper-focused on creating a better world and solving the problems of previous generations. Rather than lamenting over these issues as Generation Xers and Millennials have done, you are more interested in facing those problems head-on and together. This attitude naturally carries over into the workforce.

Analytical and Quantitative Skills

It isn't enough to have the talent and skill to find and generate information. One must also be able to analyze the resulting data to make informed decisions in the workplace. These analytical skills are also inherent to Generation Z. The U.S. educational system has put an emphasis on learning how to research and analyze information since the Boomers were in high school, but these skills have been pushed harder with each generation.

Generation Z is no different. Your secondary and post-secondary instructors of every subject pushed you to use technology to find answers and taught you how to analyze those answers for accuracy, consistency, and effectiveness. Now it is time to put those skills into effect in the workplace.

It can be difficult to show analytical and quantitative skills to an employer before you have come on board, but your resume and the interview can be used to show these strengths with practice. Focusing on projects that relied heavily on critical research and analysis, whether in school or on the job, can help you show employers that you possess these valuable skills.

Technical Skills

This is where you really shine, Gen Z. As digital natives, you possess far more experience and knowledge of technology than your predecessors. You're not afraid to learn new technologies, and you don't expect employers to teach them to you. You're willing and able to seek out these new skills for yourself.

Not only that, you are better able to adapt to new technologies. Technology has advanced at a rapid rate throughout your lifetime thus far, and you have adapted with it. As such, you are better able to pick up new technologies and apply old technology in new ways.

This ability is of great asset to employers who are not sure how to advance their companies to take advantage of new technologies. Many companies are relying on Generation Z and Millennials to come into their companies with fresh ideas and the ability to lead others to using the technology as well.

While not all Gen Zers will have these technical skills, it is far more prevalent in your generation than previous ones. Millennials lead the way in coding, especially after many picked up the skill during the pandemic. However, Gen Z has their place in this new technological working world.

If you find that you lack some of these technical skills, you're not alone. Only 36% of Generation Z has coding skills. However, it is easy to correct this through self-led courses online. Coursera is a great resource for free and cheap courses in various technological tools found in the workplace. Using these courses to learn how to best take advantage of generative AI and coworking tools will beef up your resume and further your goal of becoming an asset to the new post-pandemic workplace.

Remote Work and Communication Skills

Gen Zers often lack cross-generational and professional communication skills, as will be discussed in the next chapter. However, your generation has a leg up on others in this new remote and hybrid-remote workplace.

Because you grew up on social media, you are better able to communicate in brief than previous generations. You are more familiar with the etiquette and use of social media and similar platforms. You can use this experience via the messaging tools used by the majority of companies, such as Slack, Asana, and other coworking platforms. These tools are also easier for you to pick up than they are for older generations.

You are also a generation that learned to be productive online within a school setting, even if you attended school in person. If you went to college or high school during the pandemic, it is likely that at least some of your classes were virtual. Even in-person classes have some online elements at every grade level in today's academic settings.

This means that you have developed the ability to be self-driven and focused without supervision. This is another big asset to companies, whether you are working remotely or not. When you are able to be a self-starter and complete projects independently, you rely less on company resources and improve the company's success while positively impacting their bottom line.

Understanding how these experiences have prepared you for today's workforce is important for the interview process. These strengths should be emphasized in the interview to help employers see the benefit of hiring Generation Z employees.

End of Chapter Exercise

A SWOT analysis is an exercise in which you analyze your strengths, weaknesses, opportunities, and threats. It is often used by companies to determine whether or not a course of action is appropriate. However, job seekers can use this technique to gain a better understanding of what they have to offer employers and the pitfalls they face in the workplace.

In the next chapter, we will look at pitfalls of Gen Zers in today's workforce, with an exercise for finding your weaknesses and threats to your career. Here, we will focus on your strengths and opportunities for employment.

Feel free to use the lines provided to reflect on your answers. Alternatively, you can use your own notebook if you need more space.

Exercise 1

Using the guidance above, brainstorm your strengths and what you have to offer employers. Understanding your own strengths and weaknesses will help you better showcase those attributes in your resume and during the interview. Here are a few questions to consider while you brainstorm:

a) What apps are you familiar with that might be used in the workplace?

_____

_____

_____

_____

_____

b) Have you ever taught yourself a new piece of technology?

_____

_____

_____

_____

_____

c) Consider a time when you needed to be analytical or research for a project. Where did you shine? What tools did you use? Can you translate that to the workplace?

_____

_____

_____

_____

_____

d) Think about times in your academic career when you needed to work in a team toward a common goal. What was your role? How can experience be used in the workplace?

_____

_____

_____

_____

_____

e) What steps or tools do you use in problem-solving? How do they differ from those used by previous generations?

_____

_____

_____

_____

_____

Next, we'll take a look at the possible pitfalls that your generation faces in the workplace using these same areas of focus.

3

PITFALLS

WHILE YOUR GENERATION HAS some strengths, there are also some pitfalls of which you need to be aware. Pitfalls, in this case, are potential difficulties you may run into in today's workplace. It is entirely possible that not all of these pitfalls will apply to you. At the end of this chapter, you'll have the opportunity to explore the challenges that you need to watch out for on a personal level. For now, let's take a look at the potential pitfalls of which you need to be aware.

Lacking Professional Experience

Regardless of how prepared you feel you are for your chosen career path, there is no substitute for professional experience. Unfortunately, internships are not easy to come by, and many college students and graduates were unable to participate in internships during the pandemic. This lack of professional experience is telling in the workplace and often shows itself even during the interview process.

In previous generations, and indeed before the pandemic, estimates of how many college students participated in internships sat at around 50 to 60 percent. However, the 2021 National Survey of College Internships found that only 21.5% of college students had participated in an internship (*National Survey of College Internships 2021 Report,* 2021). If you were unable to participate in internships during or just after college, you may not have the professional experience needed for certain positions.

If this is you, there are many reasons you might not have been able to participate in internships, many of which are outside your control. According to the NSCI report, 44.2% of college students without internships reported that their internship was canceled due to the pandemic. Another 41.3% of those who did not participate in internships cited a lack of such opportunities.

In truth, not all employers offer internships, and such opportunities can be hard to come by. This is especially true in rural or underdeveloped communities. But it may not be too late. According to the National Association of Colleges and Employers, 52% of employers offered more internships in 2023 than the previous year. The average increase of intern hiring sat at 9.1 percent.

Many Gen Zers are asking, "How do I get professional experience when no one will hire me without experience?" This is a valid question and one that deserves answering. According to the Society for Human Resource Management, 61% of full-time entry-level positions require the candidate to have at least three years of professional experience (Maurer, 2018).

One of the reasons that college graduates don't participate in internships to get this experience is that there is a misconception that most internships are unpaid. However, this is no longer the case. According to the NSCI 2021 report, only 39.8% of internships are unpaid.

In addition, internships are no longer just for college students. According to Chegg Internships, about 31% of internships are taken after students graduate from college (Guterman, 2020). This trend is increasing, and it is likely that you can find paid internships to gain professional experience even if you have been out of college for a year or more.

You should carefully consider if you are lacking in the professional experience that employers are seeking, and take steps to remedy that as you are able.

Lacking Motivation and Productivity

There is a general conception of Generation Z that you are lacking in motivation and productivity. In a survey conducted by Resume Builder.com in April 2023, 71% of employers stated that Gen Z was the hardest to work with (*3 in 4 Managers Find It Difficult to Work with Generation Z,* 2023). The biggest reasons for this were a lack of motivation and productivity, as well as a lack of technical skills.

Whether or not this applies to you, it is important to understand that this is the attitude of many employers. This preconception could harm your ability to find employment, especially considering that 30% of those surveyed above who said Gen Z was the hardest to work with prefer hiring Millennials. If you want to secure your share of the work, your generation must counteract this conception with hard evidence.

As such, it is important to be prepared to show this evidence in your resume, cover letter, interview, and within your first week of hire. Adding accomplishments and highlighting projects in which you show motivation, innovation, leadership, and productivity are necessary for landing a job in today's workforce.

Another productivity pitfall that must be mentioned is the use of personal tech during work hours. Whether or not you have a habit of using your personal device while at work, the common conception among employers is that Generation Z employees are more likely to have a problem adhering to mobile phone policies. Be prepared to follow any workplace policies on cell phone use, and be prepared to address this concern if it arises in an interview.

Lacking Technical Skills

Being immersed in the digital world and comfortable with technology doesn't mean you have the technical skills employers are looking for. It is important to have an understanding and working knowledge of the tools and apps used in your industry. It is not enough to have a general understanding of technology and the capacity to learn new applications.

Employers are often unwilling to provide this training. They expect candidates to know how to use the technology utilized by their company from day one. This means that you need to research which tools are most common in your industry and learn how to use them before you apply for the job.

Luckily, there are many free courses and tutorials that will teach you how to use this technology. Some of the most widely used tools that Generation Z is lacking include:

Collaboration apps such as Asana, Slack, and Trello

Microsoft products

Adobe PDF apps

Google Suite

Conferencing and screen viewing apps like Zoom and Loom

CRM (customer resource management software)

Salesforce

Trello

Cloud storage such as Dropbox

The term "technical skills" can also refer to things like data analysis and project management, which are more difficult to prove until you are on the job. These skills should have been developed through your college coursework, particularly if you have earned or are close to a graduate degree. However, far too few Gen Zers recognized that these skills were part of the key takeaways they needed to hold onto from seemingly unrelated courses.

If you have trouble finding ways to show that you have project management, research, and data analysis skills on your resume, you probably need to consider strengthening these skills. This can be done through free and inexpensive online courses, many of which will provide a certificate upon completion. These can be added to your portfolio to prove to employers that you have these valuable skills.

Lacking Work Ethic

Generation Z is often accused of lacking a work ethic. This is often because you prioritize life and mental health over work. The first thing you must understand is that there is nothing wrong with this. As mentioned in Chapter One, you are not alone in wanting to enjoy life. Since the pandemic, even the majority of Millennials want to enjoy life more and work less.

The problem arises when you allow your personal life and mental health to impede on your work ethic. Work ethic, in this sense, refers to traits like attendance, productivity, and performance. It is okay to turn down overtime so that you can go to the concert for which you already bought tickets. It is not okay to take off work early to go to a concert with no notice.

This is an important balance that many Gen Zers don't recognize. This is largely due to the fact that you have less professional experience upon which to base a work ethic in the first place. It is one more reason why employers require prior experience for entry-level positions, and why you need to gain this experience and work ethic before launching your full-time career.

Demanding Instant Gratification

We live in a world of instant gratification. The app Temu became the most downloaded app within months of its release simply because it ate up ad space on other popular apps and offered immediate gratification of a desire.

Generation Z has always had instant gratification. No matter what you want to order, read, or view, you have access at your fingertips. You didn't have to wait for that access – you have always had it. As such, it is natural to be somewhat impatient when gratification, such as raises and performance reviews, are delayed.

The truth is that instant gratification rarely happens in the workplace. There is a certain amount of patience and hard work that must go into earning raises, projects, and promotions. If you often find yourself becoming impatient with slow-loading websites and apps, you should consciously work on cultivating patience through delayed gratification.

Lacking Communication Skills

Communication skills are sorely lacking in most Generation Z candidates. You are more likely to desire both digital and in-person communication. You are also more likely to desire frequent communication and feedback from your employer. However, your ability to communicate with other generations could be a problem.

Professional communication skills are about more than openness and honesty. You must be able to conduct yourself with a professional demeanor and use professional language. Because so much of your communication with your peers and academia is digital, your verbal and interpersonal communication skills may be lacking.

This can be a big problem in the workplace. Employers want to work with Gen Zers who can conduct themselves with the same professional decorum as older employees. If you aren't able to do that, you could be hurting yourself in the long run. Indeed, you may have trouble getting past the first interview.

Having a trusted older family member rehearse job interviews with you is one way you can build these communication skills. Ask them to be upfront and honest with you about your responses and how you are carrying yourself. Take their advice to heart, and use it in the workplace, not just in job interviews. This experience will serve you well for years to come. We'll discuss cross-generational communication in more detail in a later chapter.

End of Chapter Exercise

What pitfalls do you face, personally? It is time to brainstorm the other side of the SWOT analysis – weaknesses. Here are a few questions you should ask yourself to determine the pitfalls you need to avoid or work on to be successful in the workforce.

Exercise 1

Do you have at least three years of combined work, internship, and volunteer experience that could be applied to your chosen career field? If not, how can you gain this experience with the resources available in your area?

_____

_____

_____

_____

_____

Exercise 2

Can you prove to an employer that you are motivated and productive? How might you do that? If you don't have an answer to this one, you should initiate some volunteer or work projects to build and demonstrate these traits.

_____

_____

_____

_____

_____

Exercise 3

Are you able to critically research and analyze data? If you aren't, where can you gain some experience or education in these technical skills?

_____

_____

_____

_____

_____

Exercise 4

Are you familiar with the apps used most by companies? If not, where can you learn those skills?

_____

_____

_____

_____

_____

Exercise 5

Are you tied to your mobile phone? How long can you go without picking it up? If it is less than four hours, consider practicing going without your mobile phone for longer periods.

_____

_____

_____

_____

_____

Exercise 5

How well do you communicate with other generations? Are you familiar with professional workplace etiquette? How might you develop these skills outside the workplace?

_____

_____

_____

_____

_____

If you have completed this and the exercise from chapter one, you should have enough information to conduct your own SWOT analysis. Look at your strengths from the first exercise and consider opportunities to improve upon them. Next, look at your weaknesses from the exercise above and consider opportunities to overcome these. Finally, take a hard look at the threats to your career success that you feel helpless to improve, and consider how you will overcome them. The following chapters will give you more information on how you might do this.

Part Two: The Hunt and the Hire

The workplace isn't the only thing that has changed since the pandemic. How jobs are found and won is also changing. It can be frustrating to be told that you must "pound the pavement" looking for work, or that you must apply to every job you can find. These tactics worked for your parents, but they won't work for you.

So what does work? Let's dig in.

4

THE JOB SEARCH

T HE JOB HUNT ITSELF can be overwhelming, especially if you are in need of immediate income. When you have your parents and grandparents telling you to apply for every job you can find, it is tempting to follow their advice in the hopes that something will stick. Unfortunately, this is rarely an effective way to find a job.

Any successful job search must start with a specific goal. It is likely that your degree could be applied to more than one position, but that doesn't mean you should go after every position for which you might be qualified. You must first decide on one or two job titles that you will seek out, as well as a particular industry.

If you're not sure what your career goal should be, there are some resources to help you. The Department of Labor's Bureau of Labor Statistics publishes a free resource online each year called the Occupational Outlook Handbook. This resource gives you the ability to search for job titles to determine the requirements for that position. It will give you information about the industry, how easy it is to become employed in that industry, and what competition for those jobs might look like.

The Occupational Outlook Handbook, or OOH, is a valuable resource for targeting your job search, and one that is often overlooked. Using the OOH before starting your job hunt will ensure that your goals and qualifications are in alignment. This is important because looking for the wrong job is not likely to result in employment.

Once you have a clear career goal in mind, finding employment opportunities will be much easier. You will need to have a goal in mind before you write your resume, submit applications, and start networking. In an often-cited CareerBuilder survey from 2017, 63% of employers said they want to see a resume tailored to the position. In addition, you can't ask for a job through your professional network if you don't know what type of job to ask for.

Aside from a career goal, it is necessary to start your job search with reasonable expectations. Keep in mind that you are not likely to find a job right away. According to data from the U.S. Department of Labor, the average time to find a job as of July 2023 was 20.6 weeks, or about 5 months (*Bureau of Labor Statistics,* 2023). Of course, if you spend more than the average 11 hours per week in job search activities, including networking, your job search could take quite a bit less time. Still, according to the Bureau of Labor Statistics, the median time an individual will be unemployed is at least 8 weeks.

A clear plan is also needed. It isn't enough to draft a resume and submit it to every job that meets your goals. Experts estimate that between 70 and 85 percent of all jobs are found through networking, many of them before the position is ever posted on a job board. Many of these positions are filled by individuals who already know someone within the company.

Networking has always been an important part of any job search, but in today's job market networking has become a mandatory job search activity. You are not likely to find a position if you don't know the right people.

That doesn't mean you shouldn't submit resumes to the jobs that you really want. Instead, it means that you should back up those applications by talking with others within the same organization, or with contacts within that organization. A combination of strategies is necessary for a fast and successful job search.

It is also important to stay organized. Following up on submitted resumes and contact requests is difficult if you don't have records of who you have spoken to or where you have applied. Tracking your job search will also help you see what is working and what isn't so that you can adjust your plan accordingly.

In short, tackle your job search in the same way that you would tackle the job itself – methodically, with all of the information at hand, and by using the human and digital resources available to you.

Here is a day by day guide for the first week of your job search to help you find that perfect position. If you follow this guide and continue to follow up on the groundwork you lay within this first week, you should be able to find the right position in short order.

Day One: The Resume

The resume is an important part of your job search, even if you are using networking to find your next position. Regardless of who you know, you must have a resume tailored to the position you are seeking ready to be reviewed at a moment's notice. You will also need this resume for your LinkedIn profile and for networking groups.

There is no need to hire a professional resume writer to craft your resume. You know your experience, skills and abilities better than anyone. You should also have a good understanding of the position you are seeking and the industry in which you want to work. This knowledge arms you with everything you need to craft a tailored resume.

Start by brainstorming a list of every professional and academic experience that you have had up to this point. List out all of your duties and accomplishments for the position, including specific skills you gained or used to perform the job. Circle the items that align with your current career goals. These are the things you should highlight in your resume.

When writing about your skills and experiences, always use terminology relating to your chosen industry and career field, even if the experiences themselves were in another area. This will help recruiters see how this seemingly unrelated experience has prepared you for your desired position. It will also give you more information to put on a resume if you have not had many internships or employers since school.

One important note – never lie on a resume. The goal of a resume is to highlight how you can perform in the position and benefit the organization once hired. If you misrepresent yourself on your resume, you probably won't be keeping the job for very long.

Once you have a solid resume, you need to upload that resume to the websites used most for professional networking and job hunting. While there are many job search and networking sites, LinkedIn remains the most valuable and the most used. Your LinkedIn Profile should be easy to set up once you have your resume in hand. If you haven't already, make sure that your LinkedIn profile is linked on your resume to further enhance your network.

Day Two: Your Current Network

The best place to start networking is with the people that you already know. Make a list of every professional contact you can think of. Write down all of your academic contacts that have contacts of their own in your industry. Write down all of your social and family contacts that might be able to put you in touch with the right people to get a job.

Next, send messages to the people on your list letting them know you are looking for a new position, what position you are seeking, and the industry in which you are seeking it. Ask for advice on which networking groups to attend, and see what invites you can get to in-person networking events. Make sure that you have all of these people in your LinkedIn network, because ultimately LinkedIn is a social network for professionals. You'll see more networking opportunities, job openings, and events in your area when you include all of your professional contacts on your LinkedIn and other social media.

Day 3: LinkedIn Networking

While this step is listed as Day 3, this is actually something that you should do every day of your job search. Search on LinkedIn for professionals in your industry and send messages to at least ten different people every day. If you do this starting on Day 3, you will have reached out to 40 industry professionals asking about networking events and open positions by the end of your first week.

It is important that you do not waste your time sending connection requests and messages to random people. LinkedIn makes it easy to search for connections within your industry and the area in which you are looking for a job. You can filter by city, industry, profession, and services offered.

If you're interested in working for a particular company, searching for that company will bring up a wealth of possible connections within that organization. You don't need to look for just human resources contacts. Instead, look for connections that could be colleagues, peers, or mentors in your field.

To further build your network, make sure that your LinkedIn profile is discoverable in a search by checking your privacy settings. You should also consider posting content to your LinkedIn profile about your experiences and ideas for the industry, which shows potential employers that you are serious about your career and have the foundational knowledge and skills to be successful. Posts don't need to be long, but you should make one each day when you take the time to send your connection requests.

When you send a connection request, include a personal message about your desire to network within the industry and the position you are seeking. This will help you build your contact list and open doors in organizations. You may also get a first shot at job opportunities before they are posted.

Day 4: Industry Associations

Another great way to network for employment is through industry associations in your area. There are likely associations or informal networking groups for every industry and profession in your area. Knowing which associations and organizations support your chosen career field is vital for finding the right position and moving up in your career as you get more experience.

You should be able to identify these associations and organizations through general searches if you are familiar with your chosen industry. Most of these organizations hold frequent networking events that allow you to further expand your professional network and learn of new employment opportunities. There are also organizations that support job searches specifically, where you can get support for polishing your resume and taking steps that will help you land the right job rather than just any job.

On Day 4, find some of these associations and networking events and put at least three of them on your calendar for the next month. You can also look to Facebook and other social media to find networking groups. Meetup.com is another great place to find networking groups. Although not as popular as it once was, many groups still post their events on Meetup for older professionals.

Also on Day 4, don't forget to send out your next 10 messages or connection requests on LinkedIn.

Day 5: Alumni Organizations

Your networking journey should continue on Day 5 by contacting alumni organizations. It doesn't matter how long you have been out of school. You can always use alumni associations and events to help you get a leg up on your career search.

If you're not sure where to start, contact your college or university's academic advisory department. They will have the resources and contacts you need to get started. Your college may also have word of entry-level positions that aren't published publicly. These positions are only available to graduates of specific universities, so it is important that you establish these contacts with your school.

Ideally, you will already be involved in alumni organizations and events, but if you are not this is the time to start. Active alumni get more from their networking than those who leave school and never look back. Your college or university is a valuable source for employment, even after you have graduated. Don't discount it, even after you find that first entry-level job. University alumni events are always a great way to build and maintain your professional network.

If you do it right, the next time you are ready to look for a job you'll find your next position even faster.

Day 6: Online Job Boards

Even though most jobs are won through networking, it is still important to know what positions are available. It is possible that the perfect job is sitting on a job board. To focus your search, look for available positions on Indeed, Glassdoor, and ZipRecruiter. Other job boards might be more effective for your chosen career field. Use your best judgment.

Once you find some open positions in which you are interested, go ahead and apply for those jobs, but don't stop there. After you apply, search for that organization on LinkedIn and add some employees to your professional network. You might find that some people already in your network have contacts at these companies and can help you get your resume reviewed rather than lost in the shuffle of other applicants.

You should apply for at least three jobs and make professional contact at each organization every day for the duration of your job search. This will ensure that you are making as many contacts as possible. Even if you don't get the position you applied for, the professional contacts you make as a result could lead to other positions.

Day 7: Review Your Progress

Don't assume that what you are doing will work for you. Just as with any project, you must measure and analyze your results as you go to meet with success. Track all of the jobs that you have applied to, as well as the contacts you have made and the networking events you have attended. Look at the results and interactions that you have had in the last week, and determine if they are likely to help you find a position.

If anything doesn't seem to be working for you, adjust your plan accordingly. You may need to revisit the steps above each week to help you identify the right contacts and organizations that will help you get that next position and help you in your career moving forward.

5

INTERVIEWING

W INNING IN A JOB interview is all about making a personal connection and showing how you are the right candidate for the job. These goals might seem straightforward, but many Gen Zers have a hard time making interpersonal connections with older generations. If you are one of the 27% of Generation Z that suffers from anxiety, you may also have a hard time staying focused on the interview conversation.

Never fear, anyone can succeed in a job interview with the right preparation and mindset. There are many things you can do to ensure a successful job interview, and many of these tips will help you bridge the gap between generations as you enter the workforce as well.

Start by dressing for success. You might have heard this from older members of your family, and it still holds true today. This doesn't necessarily mean that you must arrive in a suit and tie. Be aware of the company culture and dress code and dress appropriately. You don't want to be overdressed or underdressed. Instead, plan your attire to match that of the rest of the company so that you can appear to seamlessly fit into the company's culture. When in doubt, dress in business attire.

It is also vital to remember your manners and be polite to everyone you encounter at the company, from the receptionist to the interviewer and the people you run into in between. Especially in smaller organizations, you can be sure that everyone talks to everyone else about potential candidates and visitors to the location. Make sure that what they say about you is positive.

There are three main points to remember in the interview process. You must be prepared and do your homework, you must stay calm, and you must build a personal connection with your interviewer. Let's discuss each of these in more detail before we get into how to prepare for interview questions.

Coping with Social Anxiety

Let's start with how to cope with social anxiety. Social anxiety can cause you to lose focus of the conversation and have difficulty recalling your carefully prepared answers. Generation Z is also more likely to digress from the topic at hand when asked general questions under the mantle of anxiety.

The biggest key to coping with anxiety in an interview is to focus on the present and what you can control. You cannot control the interviewer's opinion of you, nor can you control the ultimate hiring decision. However, if you have prepared carefully you can control your own answers and how they reflect on your ability to fill the role.

Grounding techniques can be invaluable during a job interview. There are several techniques that can help you remain in the present and focused on the questions at hand. The most common is the five senses technique. Identify five things you can see, four things you can hear, three things you can touch, two things you can smell, and one thing you can taste. Having a mint is a great idea in any case, but it particularly comes in handy as a grounding tool.

Another thing you can do is repeat the question to gain focus on your answer. For example, if you are asked, "What makes you unique?" you can respond with, "I am unique from other candidates because..." Even if there is a brief pause in your actual answer, this lets the interviewer know that you are considering their question and formulating a response.

The most important thing you can do to avoid anxiety in a job interview is to be prepared with your answers. When you are aware of the common interview questions and how to answer them, it helps you remain focused and on topic in the face of social anxiety.

Building a Bridge Between Your Values and Experience Regardless of the Age Gap

The chances that you will be interviewed by another member of your generation or even a Millennial are not great. It is more likely that a Gen Xer or Baby Boomer will be making final hiring decisions. As such, it is important to understand how to make a personal connection regardless of the age gap.

The most important first step in building a bridge between your values and experience and those of your interviewer is to use professional language and demeanor. When you are professional in your demeanor and answers, your interviewer will feel a deeper connection with what you have to say.

Secondly, you must be ready to talk about yourself only in relation to the role and what you have to offer the company. Older generations are focused more on work than their social life. While there will undoubtedly be an opportunity for you to share what you expect from an employer, the majority of the interview should be spent showing how you are the right candidate for the job.

Again, this requires a certain amount of preparation. It is highly recommended that you practice answering common interview questions with a member of each older generation to familiarize yourself with how each communicates. You can also use this practice opportunity to get feedback on your use of professional language and decorum.

It is also important to focus on similarities when communicating between generations. While you may be very different from your Millennial or Generation X interviewer, you will also share some similarities in interests and passions. Try to focus on these in your conversations and point out your similarities to the interviewer. This will also help show how you can integrate into the company culture.

It is also important to avoid making assumptions. Generation Z has some very negative views on Baby Boomers, of which the "Ok, Boomer" movement is the most telling. These attitudes have no place in a job interview, nor should they be present in the workplace. Instead of going into the conversation with negative assumptions, walk into the interview room ready to be accepting and show empathy for the needs of the interviewer and the company.

Finally, active listening is extremely important in bridging the gap between generations. It is far too easy to have a misunderstanding when there is a generational gap. When most people listen it is to respond, but active listening requires you to listen to understand instead. Listening to respond may seem like the obvious way to conduct yourself in a conversation in which you are answering questions, but actively listening to your interviewer may give you some clues as to how you can better make a connection and position yourself as the best candidate for the role.

Preparing for the Interview

Just as employers want to see a resume tailored to the position, so too do they want you to answer their interview questions in a way that makes your knowledge of the company obvious. You should be fully prepared to discuss the company, the position, how your experience relates to the role, and what you can bring to the company.

As such, you will need to do some homework before each interview. It isn't enough to be prepared to talk about yourself and your experience. You need to have some information about the company itself and what they envision for the position. Then, you'll need to craft your responses to make clear how you are the right candidate for the job.

This requires some preparation ahead of the interview, and you should review this preparation just before your appointment. You'll need to know the background of the company and position to answer questions such as:

Why do you want to work at this company?

What interests you about this role?

How do your skills align with this role?

Why should we hire you?

What is your salary expectation?

What can you bring to the company?

You will also need to be ready to talk about yourself in relation to the role. One of the reasons that candidates don't do well in interviews is that they talk about their experiences and skills in general terms. This is a mistake. To create a personal connection with the interviewer and the company, you need to be ready to talk about yourself in relation to the role and what you bring to the table.

It is best to use the STAR method to formulate your answers to these types of interview questions. Present the Situation, describe the Task that led to the Action and discuss the Result. Your full answer to any question should be no more than 30 seconds.

This preparation will help you answer common interview questions such as:

What makes you unique?

What motivates you?

What are your greatest strengths?

What are your greatest weaknesses?

What is your greatest accomplishment?

What are you passionate about?

The fourth interview question above is always one that causes a pause for Generation Z candidates just entering the workforce. When talking about your weaknesses, you want to be honest while also making clear that your weaknesses are actually an asset. Choose items such as "I sometimes spend too much time getting organized," which shows that you are detail oriented. Each weakness mentioned should also be a hidden strength.

Finally, you need to be ready to talk about your experience in relation to the role. This will help you answer interview questions such as:

What did you like most about your last position?

What did you like least about your last position?

Tell me about a difficult work situation and how you overcame it.

How do you respond to stress or change?

How do you handle conflict at work?

When you answer these questions, it is important to relate your answers to the culture and situations that are likely to arise when you are working for this company. This requires you to have intimate knowledge of the company and the inner workings of the position. Networking is a huge asset in this endeavor. If you have contacts at the company already, you should use those individuals to help you prepare for the interview.

Finally, there are a few open ended interview questions that you can always be ready to answer regardless of the company or position. "Tell me about yourself" is one that always catches Generation Z off-guard. What do they want to know about you? What does this have to do with your ability to perform the job? It is up to you to make that connection.

At the end of your interview, the interviewer will ask, "Do you have any questions for me?" This is your opportunity to show initiative in your career. Depending on your career goals and current education level, ask questions such as:

What professional development opportunities do you offer?

Do you offer tuition reimbursement?

Can you tell me a bit about your company culture?

What is the next step in the hiring process?

Be careful not to ask anything that has already been covered by the interviewer or that you should have been able to learn about the company before the interview. Avoid questions such as, "What does this job pay?" Questions asked for self-interests are not going to leave the interviewer with a good impression. Instead, they will think that you are only interested in what the company can offer you rather than what you can offer the company.

End of Chapter Exercise

The best way to be prepared to answer open-ended interview questions is to be prepared with something similar to an elevator pitch. An elevator pitch is a 30-second sales pitch that gives an overview of a product or service in the space of an elevator ride. You can use this same approach to prepare a 30-second answer to "Tell me about yourself."

Exercise 1

Start by brainstorming a list of interesting things about yourself, then circling everything that could relate to a position or company in which you might be interested. Then, craft a 60- to 70-word response to this question. Practice it in front of the mirror and with a friend or older family member until you are comfortable with it and can produce it on the spot without difficulty.

You can use this elevator pitch in more than just job interviews. You can use this pitch to introduce yourself in networking events to help you make the connections that will land you a job.

_____

_____

_____

_____

_____

Exercise 2

Finally, do this same exercise again but in response to the question, "Walk me through your resume." The interviewer will already have your resume in front of them. What they really want to know is what you think about your career thus far and where you are taking it, as well as how their company and the open position fit into that plan. This too should be a 30-second response, and one that can be used again and again in interviews and networking.

_____

_____

_____

_____

_____

6

GETTING HIRED

T HERE ARE SOME THINGS about entering the workforce that have not changed in many years. One of the biggest mistakes candidates make when they are first entering the workforce is in thinking that the interview is the last interaction before the hire. This isn't just true of Generation Z. This has been a common pitfall for every generation entering the workforce. TheThe simple fact of the matter is that follow up is required if you want to win the job.

The job market is very competitive, and companies often interview a minimum of six people before they hire for a position. The more people the company interviews for the role, the less likely you are to win the job. It is important to keep your interview fresh in the mind of those making hiring decisions.

Generation Z has a harder time making follow up calls and emails than previous generations. You have more social anxiety and have more difficulty promoting yourself to others. You are likely less confident overall, especially if you have remained unemployed for some time or have less internship experience than other candidates. You must not let that self-doubt affect your job search.

Getting hired after the interview requires several steps that should not be skipped in your job search. Even if you have other interviews lined up, it is necessary to follow up with each company with which you have applied if you want to get the right job.

Your first step is to thank the interviewer for meeting with you. This thank you note can be a quick email sent a day or two after the interview. If you were the first interview of the process, this email will ensure that you remain in the mind of the interviewer over those that they have spoken to since your meeting.

Here is a sample email to give you an idea of what to include, but keep in mind that this should be tailored to the position and the actual interview held.

Dear (Name),

Thank you for the opportunity to interview for the (position) role in your company. I enjoyed discussing my experience and how it can benefit your company. In our interview, we discussed how my internship experiences have prepared me for this specific role. I hope that you provide me with the opportunity to show you first hand how this experience can benefit your company.

I look forward to the next steps in the hiring process. Thank you again.

If you got the job interview through networking, reach out to your other contacts at the company as well. Thank them for helping you get the interview opportunity and ask them if they have heard any news about filling the position. It is simply good manners to thank your contacts for their help, and it helps keep your network strong in case you need to keep searching. They might also be able to give you inside information about the hiring process, what you can expect, and whether or not there are additional steps you should take.

Talking to your contacts in your professional network will also help you stay fresh in the minds of the hiring managers. Those contacts can make their own inquiries and make mention of your interview when they talk to their superiors or the hiring managers. This can go a long way toward helping you win the job, because when you already have contacts at the company that are trusted by those making hiring decisions advocating for you it makes you look like a more viable candidate.

In chapter five we discussed briefly the need to ask about the hiring process. This is important because you need to know what to expect and when to follow up with the interviewer. If the interviewer told you that they would be interviewing for the position for another week after your meeting, you should follow up with a second email at the end of that week reminding them of your application.

When you follow up this second time, you need to reestablish the personal connection you made in the interview. Make sure that the interviewer knows that you are still interested in the position, and why. Remind them how your experience relates to the role, and make mention of something that you discussed in the interview that will make them remember the interaction fondly.

Here is a sample email you might send after all interviews are held.

Dear Name,

Thank you for meeting with me on (Date) to discuss the (role) position available in your company. During our interview, you mentioned that the hiring process would move to the next step this week. I wanted to thank you again for meeting with me, and reiterate my interest in the position.

During our interview, you mentioned that you need someone in this role that will take initiative and meet hard deadlines. I posit that there is no better candidate for this position based on my experience with (company) and the results I achieved there. (Remind them of this achievement.)

Thank you again for the interview opportunity. I look forward to hearing from you with the next steps.

A third followup is rarely warranted, unless you have been contacted by the company for a second interview or the next steps in the hiring process. With each step and barrier won, you should send another follow up to keep your candidacy fresh in their minds. Remember that you are competing with others for this position, and the mind is a fickle thing. If another candidate has similar experience and skills, but interviews after you do, they are more likely to win the position if you don't keep your interview fresh in the hiring manager's mind.

At the same time, you don't want to be a pest or harass the interviewer or the company in seeking the position. This can be as damaging as not following up at all. There is a delicate balance that must be achieved. Following these guidelines will help you tremendously in those efforts.

Most companies have a multi-step interview process in which you interview with progressively important individuals within the company. Follow up with each of these individually after the interview rather than sending an email to all contacts in the company. The last person with whom you interviewed will be discussing the role with other decision makers, and there is no need to continuously follow up with every contact at the company.

At the same time, it is important not to put all of your eggs in one basket. What seemed like a great interview could lead nowhere. Keep applying for jobs, keep networking, and keep interviewing for other positions. Ideally you will have more than one job offer on the table from which to choose your new career.

When you are at last contacted with a job offer, make sure you understand everything that relates to that offer. Compare job offers carefully, and don't be afraid to pit companies against one another. If two companies are equally interested in hiring you, let them compete with each other to give you the best compensation package.

However, it is important not to become cocky in these interactions. Make sure that you keep yourself grounded and have realistic expectations. When the final job offer comes across the table, be ready to either accept it or walk away.

Accepting the job offer isn't the end of the hiring process. Although it was not common for some time, references and background checks have once again become the norm. Make sure that you have a list of references that will speak highly of you, and all of these should be from your professional network. They should be individuals that are familiar with your skills, abilities, and work ethic.

Background checks are a formality for most people, but if there is anything that might come up on a background check that could jeopardize your chances you should be proactive and let the company know ahead of time what to expect. You have a better chance of advocating for yourself if you are honest and upfront than if something arises that jeopardizes your candidacy after the fact.

Most companies have an onboarding process and some may have a probationary period. It is important to remain professional and courteous throughout this process, because it could be stopped at any time. The company undoubtedly has other qualified candidates to choose from, and there is no reason to jeopardize your chances when you are so close to the finish line.

In truth, you should always conduct yourself in the workplace as though you are being interviewed for a new position. This attitude will serve you well as your career progresses. It will position you to take on new roles within the same company, earn promotions, and further your career. It will also help you make personal connections that will build your professional network, which is so important for a career search later on down the road.

Finally, be sure that you are honest in all of your paperwork and onboarding with the company. If you were honest in the interview and on your resume, this should be a simple matter. Never misrepresent yourself and be prepared for every step of the process. Have your identification documents ready for the necessary federal hiring paperwork, and make sure that you have all information needed when you arrive.

7

NAVIGATING A NEW WORKPLACE

N AVIGATING A NEW WORKPLACE can be challenging for Gen Zers. One of the characteristics of your generation is that you have more anxiety than older employees at the company. You're likely to feel a lot of nervousness, and you might have feelings of inadequacy. The best way to combat these is through careful preparation.

In addition, most employers expect you to prove yourself rather quickly. According to a study by Robert Half Finance and Accounting, 54% of employers expect you to prove yourself in one to two months, and 9% of employers give even less time than that (Robert Half, 2016). As such, you need to be prepared to give your new workplace your best from day one.

To make matters worse, Gen Zers often feel pressured to figure things out for themselves. You don't want to ask questions in fear that you will have been expected to already know the answer. However, it is important to remember that your inexperience and youth were already known to the employer before they hired you. They know you are new to the workforce, and as such may have questions that the average employee might not have.

If you're not comfortable asking your manager or supervisor to help, turn to your coworkers. Your peers and colleagues are your best resource for learning a new position and company without asking too many questions of your supervisor. Turning to your colleagues is, in itself, inherently resourceful. As such, employers will recognize that you are, essentially, figuring things out for yourself.

You should also take this opportunity for professional development and learn new technical tools on your own, if possible. If your manager hasn't specifically mentioned training in any of the tools you are presented within your new role, you should plan to figure these out for yourself.

Because Generation Z are considered digital natives, employers expect you to be able to pick up any new SaaS, app, or software at the drop of a hat. However, this doesn't come that easily to all Gen Zers. If you're one of those who doesn't pick up new technology quickly, you may need to be prepared to spend some personal time learning it for yourself. You can do this at work when you don't have other tasks to complete, or you can learn the software at home through online tutorials.

Even with all of these potential pitfalls and anxiety-inducing situations, it is important not to feel overly anxious or overwhelmed as you enter a new workplace. Generation Z as a whole has more issues with anxiety and feelings of inadequacy than any other generation. As such, you need to be self-aware and prevent those feelings from wreaking havoc as you start your new job.

Part of this self-care is being aware that you will make mistakes. Even seasoned candidates with years of experience make mistakes on the first day or two of employment as they learn the ins and outs of a new company with new policies and procedures to discover. Making mistakes is fine, it is how you handle them that makes the difference.

If you are too anxious and are having a difficult time seeing your self-worth, mistakes on the job can be derailing to your entire day. It is so important that you don't allow this to happen. Use your breaks to your advantage, taking time to recenter yourself and prepare for the next part of your day. It can be tempting to spend your breaks getting to know your new coworkers, but taking that time for yourself is much more important in the first days of employment.

Instead of allowing mistakes to make you feel inadequate, use them as learning experiences. Apologize for the mistake, and don't feel the need to justify why you made it. Instead, let your supervisor know you have acknowledged the mistake, and tell them how you will avoid it in the future. This also gives them the opportunity to let you know if there is something about the assignment or task that you have misunderstood. Handling mistakes in this way will help you learn more, make a good impression, and maintain your mental health.

There are many things you can do to make your first days and weeks in a new workplace an ultimate success. It all starts with being prepared, being aware of your shortcomings, handling mistakes with care, and being prepared to figure out some things on your own. Here is a brief day-by-day guide to navigating a new workplace.

Before Your First Day

Navigating a new workplace requires the same type of networking you used to get the job. Making connections in your new workplace will give you valuable resources and support as you learn the company and the position that you have been given. Start your new work experience by investigating the company culture on their social media accounts and making connections on LinkedIn and other social media with your new coworkers. Introduce yourself in your connection request. This will go a long way toward helping you find a mentor as well, which we will cover in the next part of this book.

You should also reach out to human resources and make sure that you have all of the information you need for your first day. Discuss the dress code, if you have not already gleaned this for yourself from your previous research for the interview. Obtain a copy of the employee handbook, if there is one, and any other onboarding documents you are allowed to have before arriving for your first day. You will be better prepared if you review these items ahead of time. If the company has a policy against providing this outside of the office, you will at least have shown initiative and a desire to follow company policy.

When you are hired, or a few days before your first day, reach out to your new manager as well. Ask about their expectations for the first few days and weeks of your employment. Knowing what is expected of you can help you feel more confident in meeting those requirements.

Finally, prepare for your first day. Make sure you have your clothing chosen and laid out, and that you have run through your morning routine to ensure you have enough time to get ready and get to work. You should even practice and time your morning commute on a weekday at the time you will normally be traveling just to ensure you have given yourself ample time to compensate for traffic.

The Day Before Your First Day

Depending on how much time you have had to prepare for your new workplace, by the day before you start your new job you should be fairly ready for tackling the new job. But there are still a few things you should do before you go in for your first day to help make your experience as stress-free and enjoyable as possible.

Your new coworkers are invaluable resources in helping you get ahead in your new role. It is most helpful if you can make connections with employees that have already worked in the role in which you have taken. This will give you valuable insights into your job and what is expected of you.

The best way to take advantage of this resource is to make connections early. At the same time, you don't want to waste valuable work time trying to network and learn new coworkers. To achieve a happy medium, create yet another 30-second elevator pitch that you can use to introduce yourself to other employees on your first day. This elevator pitch should include who you are, the role you have taken in the company, where you used to work or where you graduated from college, and a fun fact or two. Doing this the day before your first day on the job will keep it fresh in your mind without the need to practice, which can make your pitch sound rehearsed.

On your first day you may be invited to lunch. Make sure you are prepared with lunch money so that you can accept any invitation and not worry about how you are going to pay. If this is your first job or you have been out of work for a while, coming up with cash for lunch can be daunting. Plan ahead and have it ready the day before you start work.

Finally, make sure you get a good night's sleep the day before you start your new job. Self care is an important part of being a good employee. You cannot function at your best if you don't take care of yourself. Eat a good dinner and go to bed early. You'll thank yourself for it the next day.

On Day One

It is a good idea to always plan to arrive at work early, but this is especially true of your first day. You'll need to make sure you know where to go, where to find your manager, where your workstation is, and how to clock in for the day. Plan to arrive at least 15 minutes early to show initiative and be ready to work at your start time.

Put your phone on silent for this first day of work, even if your company allows personal mobile use during work hours. Unless you must have the phone to work, turn it off and leave it put away so that you don't have any added distractions. Your nervousness and the overwhelming amount of information you are taking in make it difficult to focus, and you want to remain present as much as possible while learning your new position and company.

Take a notebook with you on your first day. You're going to be thrown a lot of information very quickly. Some of it will be for your information only, but much of it will relate to your role and the company's expectations. Make sure that you write down anything that might seem important. You can review your notes and remove any pages that are not necessary for completing your job when you get home at the end of the day. Plan on keeping this notebook with you for at least the first week of the job.

It is easy to be overwhelmed, but you still need to pay attention to your surroundings as well. Take careful note of anything related to company culture that might affect your work performance or how you are viewed by management. Make sure that you are conforming to this company culture and any unwritten rules, such as when to converse with fellow employees.

The best way to avoid being overwhelmed is to ask lots of questions, and write down the answers as appropriate. Make sure you understand everything relating to your role in the company. While many people will say that the only stupid question is the one not asked, you do want to avoid asking anything that should be blatantly obvious or that you can figure out on your own. Still, asking questions when something is unclear is better than making mistakes later.

Finally, listen and observe more than you speak. As a generation, you are more likely to overexplain and talk when you are nervous or in an uncomfortable situation. It is important not to do this on your first day. This day is all about learning, which means that you need to listen and pay attention to everything going on around you. At the same time, avoid being too quiet. Your manager expects some feedback and questions if you are to be successful.

The End of Your First Day

If you want to be truly successful, you will need to do a bit of homework at the end of your first several days. At the end of your first day, review your notes and make a list of questions for your supervisor when you return to work the next day. If you identified any new technical tools that the company uses that you are unfamiliar with, develop a plan to get familiar with these tools.

Most employers do not train employees in these tools, but expect them to know them already or be able to pick them up on their own. If that describes the company you now work for, you will need to be proactive in learning this software. Most of the tools that companies use are available for personal use and there are tutorials through the software companies to help you learn them.

There are also free and inexpensive courses on websites like Corsera and Udemy that will help you get familiar with these tools. You won't be able to learn them in one night, but you will be able to make a plan to get ahead. This way if you struggle in your first week, you can let your supervisor know your plan so that they can rest assured that you will be up to speed in short order.

Finally, try to get some sleep. Your second day is likely to be just as intensive as the first, and you want to be fully prepared. You can repeat these tips for each day of your first week.

Your First Weekend Off

Your first days off after starting a new job should be relaxing, but you also need to prepare for your next week. Your first order of business is to take care of yourself. Make plans with some friends for Saturday and enjoy a good dinner. Take some time for yourself and reward yourself for your progress thus far. This is as important to your success as the preparation you should do on Sunday.

On Sunday, you need to prepare for the next week of your employment. Spend several hours playing with or learning the tools you need for the new role. Review all of your notes from the first week so that everything is fresh in your mind. Make a list of questions, suggestions, or affirmations you want to go over with your supervisor Monday morning.

Finally, go to bed early and get some rest. Sleep is so important for recovering and preparing for the trying experience of starting a new job and proving yourself as quickly as possible.

PART 3: NAVIGATING THE TRADITIONAL WORKPLACE

One of the reasons Generation Z has such anxiety about entering the workforce is that you don't feel comfortable in the traditional workplace. You believe that the world can be better than those traditional views. And that's okay. You should want and strive for a better world.

But there is a happy medium between being a maverick and walking that traditional line. It is very important to find that balance early on in your career. You will be able to make greater impacts as a result.

To start understanding how you can navigate and improve upon the traditional workplace, let's start by discussing mentorship within your company.

8

EMBRACING MENTORSHIP

N AVIGATING A NEW WORKPLACE or career is much easier when you have a mentor. Understanding the importance of mentorship is vital to your career, but that need shouldn't equate to just walking up to the oldest member of your new group of coworkers and asking, "Will you be my mentor?" There is much more to it than this, or at least, there should be.

Mentorship is vital to both your success in the new company and your career as a whole. Many companies have mentorship programs in which they initiate one-on-one and group mentorship opportunities precisely because they understand this need. However, while these mentorship opportunities are valuable, they do not take the place of a personal mentor. In truth, you should have more than one mentor throughout your career, often at the same time.

Having a mentor in the workplace who has been with the company for a while and can help you with the ins and outs of the organization and industry is important, but it isn't the only mentorship you need. There are actually several different types of mentors that you will encounter throughout your career, and you should take advantage of all mentorship opportunities within and outside of your current organization.

The traditional mentor is someone older and wiser who has been working in the company and industry for a while. Perhaps they even worked in your role, or a similar one in another company earlier in their career. Most people think of traditional mentors as being the most senior members of the team or company, but this isn't always the case. In a multi-generational workplace in which members of each generation are represented throughout the company's hierarchy, traditional mentors may not be that much older than you. Millennials, for example, make great traditional mentors.

Traditional mentorship is important because these mentors are a guiding light to help you navigate the new company, the new position, and the new career as a whole. They will help you see your mistakes before and after you make them, learn from those mistakes, and prevent them from negatively affecting your career.

Traditional mentors are there to help you make your way up that ever-changing and growing corporate ladder. While a traditional mentor does not necessarily need to come from your own company, you should have a traditional mentor in your workplace to help you avoid the pitfalls that we discussed at the beginning of this book. There is nothing wrong with having more than one traditional mentor, with one being outside your company and one within.

The second type of mentor that you might want to look for is an affinity mentor. This type of mentor is particularly important to a diverse workforce. Women mentor women, people of color mentor the same, and so on. The importance of an affinity mentor is that each diverse group of the workforce has faced their own challenges in climbing up the corporate ladder of their careers. Even though Generation Z is pushing for change, the traditional workplace still holds those challenges. An affinity-based mentor can help you cope with these more social aspects of your career.

Finding an affinity mentor within your company will likely be difficult. It really depends on the diversity of your workplace. However, there are many networking and professional groups that will give you the perfect opportunity to find an affinity mentor. It's a good idea to find someone who is in an older generation for this type of mentorship.

Generation X affinity mentors are ideal. Baby Boomers had to struggle much more than you will, Gen Z. Generation X also struggled more than you will, but they are more familiar with your age group and interests. This unique Gen X/GenZ relationship will allow you to appreciate how much easier you have it than previous generations while still benefiting from valuable advice that will help you in your own diverse career.

Third, you should find a peer mentor, also called a mirror mentor. A peer mentor is a mentor who is close to your own age but has been within the company and workforce a bit longer than you. These peers have valuable insight as to how to avoid mistakes and move up in your career while having a complete understanding of your generation and actual traits and characteristics. Peer mentors should not be undervalued, and they should almost always come from within your company. These peer mentors can become valuable networking contacts when you switch to another company and get a new peer mentor.

Finally, you need to find a cross-functional mentor in your workplace. This mentor should come from another department or organization that you work with on a regular basis. They should be familiar with your position, but probably never held it themselves. They should be familiar with your generation, but be from another generation entirely.

The main purpose of having a cross-functional mentor in your company is to have a different perspective on work situations and assignments. It is much easier to be objective when the outcome has no direct impact on you or your job. That is what a cross-functional mentor is all about.

Now that you understand the types of mentors and which generations they are likely to be, let's discuss how to actually find and initiate a mentorship. Imagine that you have started at a new company and you want to find a mentor. You see the senior member of your workplace who is not your immediate supervisor and ask them to be your mentor at the water cooler at the end of your first week. What will happen?

Likely, the individual will shoot you down, develop a poor opinion of you, and laugh about the encounter as soon as you walk away. If you are unlucky, the laughter might begin before you ever leave the area, and it might come from others standing nearby at the time you asked.

The truth is that mentorship isn't something that can just happen. You need to build a relationship with the other generations in your workplace before you ask them to mentor you. Mentor/mentee relationships often begin without any formal ask, but simply through the mutual understanding and natural development of the working relationship.

At the same time, you can't be afraid to ask for mentorship, especially if you are looking for mentors outside your workplace. You have to be willing to ask for that mentoring relationship if it isn't offered. Many people who would make great mentors would never think of filling that role until they are asked. The worst thing that could happen is that they will say no, especially if you have taken the time to build a rapport before asking.

How do you build a relationship with a potential mentor? Spend some time really getting to know them. This is a good rule in general for finding a mentor because you can't know that they are the right person to guide you if you don't know much about them. It is especially important to get to know peer and affinity mentors before initiating a mentorship relationship.

Update your potential mentors on your progress in your company, position, and career, while also asking to stay updated on their own achievements. You can also build and maintain a relationship with a mentor by remembering that it is a two-way street. You need to offer to help your mentor as much as you ask for their help. Then, express gratitude for their guidance and assistance in your own endeavors, and for the opportunity to help them for a learning experience.

If you have trouble finding a mentor, you have several options. You can join mentorship groups, but the best way to find a mentor is through the professional networking groups and events discussed in Chapter 4 and used during your job search. Professional networking is so important for this and other reasons. These mentors and the others you meet through networking can help you along your journey to a better future in your chosen career path. You never know what opportunities they might lead to, and therefore this is an important place to look for a mentor. These networking groups are often the best place to find affinity mentors.

Remember that having more than one mentor is important. You should have a mentor from each generation. A Baby Boomer mentor will be able to help you navigate a traditional workplace. A Generation X mentor will be ideal as an affinity mentor. A Millennial is an ideal traditional mentor in the workplace, especially when they have previously worked in your position within the same company. And, finally, a peer mentor from Generation Z that is slightly older or more experienced than you are is a big help when you are championing diversity and inclusion in the workplace while bringing new and innovative ideas to the table.

End of Chapter Exercise

Exercise 1

Brainstorm what you want to look for in each type of mentor. What qualities do you want to look for? What affinities do you want to find? From which generation should each mentor be? What do you want from each mentoring relationship?

_____

_____

_____

_____

_____

Exercise 2

Next, make a plan for finding mentors. Which type of mentor will you look for in which places? What types of mentors are you likely to find in your current workplace? What other organizations or networking groups might present the right opportunity for a mentor?

_____

_____

_____

_____

_____

9

EFFECTIVE COMMUNICATION ACROSS GENERATIONS

T HERE IS NO DOUBT that each generation has its own communication styles and preferences, and you will be working with people
from all generations in today's workforce. While the Silent Generation
only makes up about 10% of the workforce, Baby Boomers, Generation
X, and Millennials make up the majority of it. You, Gen Zer, are
currently outnumbered, and you must learn to alter your communication
style to effectively communicate across generational gaps.

Effective communication is one of the most important skills you
can develop for any career. Every workplace is different, but the basics
of interpersonal communication remain the same. Even when communicating across generations, remembering the basics of interpersonal
communication learned in your high school and college courses will
serve you well.

Still, there are some challenges to communicating across generations.
Each generation has its own characteristics and communication styles.
However, in the workplace, these often converge to a neutral, profes-
sional effort.

Studies have found that the biggest obstacle to cross-generational
communication is preconceived notions of each generation (Downs,
2019). In short, the stereotypes with which you associate each generation
have a large impact on how you communicate with them. It is necessary

to put these stereotypes and preconceived notions aside if you want to communicate effectively in the workplace and have your ideas heard.

For example, consider the stereotypes that you associate with Baby Boomers or the traditional workforce. About 25% of Baby Boomers are still working, making up about 19% of the total workforce. These individuals are most likely to be business owners and upper management. It is these individuals, along with Generation X, that are likely to be making hiring decisions as well.

Generation Z has a generally poor view of Baby Boomers. The term "OK, Boomer" has been trending for some time. Gen Zers tend to believe that Boomers are set in their outdated ways and are unwilling to change their minds or hear new ideas. Baby Boomers are often thought to be self-centered, unrealistic, political, and power-driven. But this is only one side of the story.

The truth is that many Baby Boomers are open to the ideas of Gen Zers like you. Why? Because they understand that their knowledge of this technical world is not the same as yours. They may be set in their ways and their views of the world, but that doesn't mean they aren't willing to listen to your ideas in the workplace. If you think about Generation X, you'll find that the stereotype of being impatient and cynical is also incongruent with the Gen Xers that you have known in school and the workplace.

Essentially, you must put these stereotypes aside and focus instead on how each of these generations communicates. When you communicate in a way that makes sense to the person you are trying to reach, you have a much higher chance of a successful conversation.

When talking to Baby Boomers, you must remember that they have experience you don't have. Instead of presenting your ideas in a matter-of-fact manner, ask them what they have tried before, what has worked, and what hasn't worked over time. Then, you can adjust your presentation to show them how your ideas or project plan overcomes those obstacles.

However, this approach doesn't work when you are talking to Generation X. Gen Xers expect you to get straight to the point. They want you to be clear, direct, and concise. They want to know the pros and cons of what you are presenting to them, and why you think it would be the right course of action. Then, they want you to sit back and listen to their point of view. Communications with Generation X need to be more of a give-and-take.

As a Gen Zer, you are more likely to communicate effectively with Millennials. Millennials have spent most of their lives in the same technological frenzy that you have known since you were born. Show respect by asking them their opinions and ideas, but don't be afraid to share your own either. You can be a bit more informal when communicating with Millennials, but they are still going to appreciate a professional tone.

Of course, these are generational generalizations that may not apply to every one of that age group. The best way to communicate across generations is to become an effective communicator in general. There are several strategies you can use to improve your communication skills with any generation. Follow these strategies to put your career on the fast track in the workplace.

Mirroring

Mirroring is your best tool in communicating across generations. Using the mirroring technique in interpersonal communication requires you to pay close attention to the body language, tone, and style of the person you are communicating with and adapt to it accordingly. This is the best way to get used to talking to different members of different generations.

Active Listening

Active listening is another important part of communicating across generations. When you allow stereotypes to affect your communication style, active listening often goes by the wayside. As a Gen Zer, it is tempting to listen to Baby Boomers or Gen Xers simply to respond. Active listening requires you to listen for understanding, with the response being a secondary reaction. You must engage in active listening for effective mirroring in communication.

Eye Contact

Don't be afraid to make eye contact while you are talking to older generations. Rather than seeming too forward, making eye contact in the workplace is a sign of respect and openness. Baby Boomers and some members of Generation X may expect eye contact as a form of respect, and if you don't give that respect in a way that they recognize they will be unlikely to listen to what you have to say.

Empathy

See the situation from the other person's point of view, and react empathetically. You can be empathetic and still disagree with the other person. Empathy is best practiced in the workplace by acknowledging the problem and offering a unique or forward-thinking solution. If you handle cross-generational conversations with empathy rather than stereotypes, you will have much more effective conversations.

10

Owning Your Career Path

T HE TRADITIONAL WORKPLACE CAN feel stifling for Gen Zers. As the youngest generation in the workforce, you might feel as though your career is at the mercy of those who came before you. It is important that you not get wrapped up in this way of thinking. Taking control of your own career path, both at your new company and going forward, is vital for your eventual success.

You might expect that your employer would invest in your professional development, but this is not always the case. According to survey studies from People Keep, 40% of employers don't offer professional development programs (Charaba, 2022). In addition, the Department of Labor reports that only 30.9% of employees receive professional and technical skill development training from their employer (Bureau of Labor Statistics, 2023).

While your company is more likely to offer training in communication skills and the computer software needed to perform your duties within that company, it is also unlikely that you will stay with the same employer indefinitely. Whereas Baby Boomers and even Generation Xers once expected to stay at their employer for a long time, you know from watching your parents that this isn't the case. Not every company has opportunities for advancement. In fact, the median tenure, or the average amount of time one person has been with the same employer, is only about 4 years (Bureau of Labor Statistics, 2022).

It is also true that many of the skills and lessons you need to advance your career can only be learned on the job. That experience is valuable in itself, and you should make every mistake and new skill a lesson to remember. If you have a hard time living in the moment, practice jotting down a note each time you learn something new. Reviewing your notes once a week will help you remember those lessons later and apply them to your current and future positions.

Still, there is much that you will need to learn on your own. Thankfully, your generation being digital natives gives you an advantage over the generations that came before you. While the career and skill development opportunities available to you are available to all generations, you have access to this wonderful world of education at the very infancy of your career. This means that if you take control of your own destiny, you can more easily move up in a career faster than your parents or grandparents did.

The first step in taking control of your career is to decide where you want that career to go. What are your ultimate career goals? Next, you must determine what is required to reach those goals. Finally, you must go after those smaller goals and complete the steps to meet your goal.

Career goals should be made using the SMART method. Goals should be Specific, Measurable, Achievable, Relevant, and Timebound. Career goals should then be broken down into smaller goals, such as a specific position you will seek out or training that you must complete. Each of these smaller goals will be broken down into steps. This helps keep you focused and making progress toward career advancement.

An example of a specific career goal would be that you want to be a computer programmer. The goal is measurable because it will be very clear when you have reached that goal and the smaller goals that lead up to it. The goal should be achievable, meaning that you have the skills or aptitude to obtain the career. The goal should be relevant in that it should have something to do with your prior education or experience.

Finally, the goal should be timebound, which means that you must set a time by which you will meet the goal.

As you can see, creating a career plan is much more complex than simply deciding what you want to be when you grow up. A career plan is made up of a variety of stair-stepped positions, training, and education that leads naturally to the ultimate career goal. It requires careful thought and research.

One of the best tools at your disposal for developing a career plan is the Department of Labor. There are two primary tools you can use to own your career and advance accordingly to meet your life goals. The first is the Occupational Outlook Handbook, located at http://www.bls.gov/ooh. This free tool allows you to search for any career and any position within a career field so that you can easily see the natural progression of working in the field and what is required to advance.

The second tool is the free self-assessment tool found through the OOH called O*Net. This free tool allows you to discover your basic aptitudes and skills and the careers that are best suited for them. The tools allow you to find careers based on the education, skills, and training that you have already received, which is helpful if you have earned a broader degree.

Once you have a clear understanding of the career you want and how to get there, you can begin laying out the plan itself based on your resources and what is available in your area.

End of Chapter Exercise

Exercise 1

Create a 3-year career plan, including the position you want to have at the end of the three years and what is needed to get there. How will your current position help you advance and meet your goals in three years? What training or education do you need to complete to reach your three-year career goal? How will you get that training or develop those skills? Will you need to look for a position in another company, or will you have advancement opportunities where you are?

Creating a three-year career plan requires quite a bit of thought and research, but taking the time to do this now and revisiting the plan every six months to see how you have progressed will help you stay on track and own your career path.

_____

_____

_____

_____

_____

Exercise 2

Finally, consider where you want to be in five years. Where do you want to be in ten years? Twenty years? It is fun to dream and it is a good idea to have some clue as to where you want your life to go, but these longer plans should be made with caution. Remember that technology, particularly AI, is still advancing at a rapid rate, and the course of your career could be at the mercy of this technology and other societal and economic changes.

_____

_____

_____

_____

_____

PART 4: DISRUPTING THE STATUS QUO

As we already discussed, part of Gen Z's magic is being able to disrupt the status quo. You see things in a way that other generations do not. Even though other generations see the need for change, none have been as motivated to bring that change into reality than Generation Z. What's more, employers and colleagues from other generations will expect you to disrupt the status quo and may cheer you on from the sidelines, even if they do so silently.

How do you disrupt the status quo? Glad you asked! Let's dig in, shall we?

11

CHAMPIONING DIVERSITY AND
INCLUSION

I N THE first PART of this book, we discussed that Generation Z is
the most diverse of all generations in the workforce. The very fact
that your generation is more diverse explains why you are more likely
to champion diversity and inclusion in the workplace. While diversity
and inclusion is improving year over year, many people agree that it is
not moving forward fast enough to make a significant difference for
millions of Americans.

Diversity and inclusion in the workplace are important because
many Americans find it difficult to find employment or are paid
less than white males in the workplace. This is a proven fact shown
through the stats from the Bureau of Labor Statistics. As of 2021, 23%
of the workforce is diverse, meaning that they are other than white
males (Bureau of Labor Statistics, 2021). However, unemployment
rates for people of color are more than 3% higher than the national
average.

Meanwhile, gender also plays a role in workforce participation.
Only 52% of women participate in the workforce, with the unemployment rate about the same as people of color (Bureau of Labor Statistics,
2022). Keep in mind that the unemployment rate is how many people
are unemployed and looking for work, but does not necessarily include
people who are not and have never filed for unemployment benefits.

Finally, sexual orientation also affects workplace diversity. Workers identifying as part of the LGBTQ+ community are more likely to report loss of employment, with 29% of transgender survey respondents saying that they lost employment between July 2021 and April 2022 (Center for American Progress, 2022). This is perhaps the worst disparity when it comes to diversity and inclusion, but Generation Z itself has more LGBTQ+ members than any other generation. This clearly shows why you are in the best position to effect change in this area of your workplace.

In fact, Generation Zer, you are the future of hope for diversity and inclusion. A survey by Pew Research found that you are more likely to consider diversity and inclusion efforts a good thing, with 68% of workers from 18 to 29 believing this (Minkin, 2023). The majority of all workers (58%) also believe that inclusion efforts are a good thing, but the percentage of the workforce that thinks this way decreases with each age group. Unfortunately, this study did not examine the data strictly by generation, but only 46% of those aged 50 to 64 believed that diversity initiatives were a good thing.

Even though older generations aren't likely to consider diversity and inclusion in the workplace, they are expecting your generation to be more accepting of all and more diverse in general. They also expect you to speak out about these things more freely than past generations. It is up to you to take advantage of these expectations to try to drive change in your organization and in society as a whole.

Fostering diversity and inclusion in the workplace is not always easy, but it begins with speaking up when you notice disparities in the workplace. If you notice that a man received a promotion when a woman was more qualified, you should speak up and bring your concern to the awareness of the human resources department, if there is one. If your organization doesn't have a human resources department, discuss it with the supervisor of the individual who made the hiring decision. You should do the same if you see a person of color passed over for promotion, or learn that they are being paid less than their white male counterparts.

Driving change in diversity and inclusion also requires speaking up when there are disciplinary actions, harassment in the workplace, or other disparities that are often ignored by those not involved. It is up to you to push management and business owners to include everyone on equal terms. This is best done by pointing out the ways that diverse colleagues contribute to the team, the company, and society as a whole. This can be done in numerous ways depending on how your company organizes and works within teams.

Here are a few more ways you can drive change and push society and the workforce to be more inclusive.

Recommend Diverse Employees

Whether you are recommending someone you think would be a perfect addition to the team or you want to see someone be promoted within the ranks, make your recommendations known to those who make the decisions. As a younger employee, your opinions and recommendations may not seem to make an impact. However, simply by recommending diverse employees and candidates you can bring these issues to the attention of those making hiring and promoting decisions. In this way, you make them think about their decision and the criteria being used more carefully and with inclusion in mind.

Celebrate Differences and Inclusion

The best way to celebrate differences and inclusion is to meet regularly with other employees and colleagues in an informal setting that allows you to explore how you are different and how you can better work together for an inclusive workplace. Some employers have mixers and other informal team-building events that help facilitate this inclusion, but if your employer doesn't subscribe to such events you can create your own.

Speak Up About Pronouns and Preferred Names

There are many situations in which an individual may wish to use specific pronouns or a preferred name, and not all of them are related to sexual orientation. If you know that someone has a preferred name or pronouns and you see that those are not being used, speak up and back up that individual by telling others to use their preferred name and pronouns. Being supportive of diverse employees, especially when you are not identifying as diverse yourself, can have big impacts regardless of your age group.

Think About How You and Others Communicate

Do you communicate with inclusion? Do others in your workplace communicate with inclusion? Make sure that you are accepting of diversity in your conversations with other employees, and speak up when you notice that someone else is not doing so. How you talk to and about people matters, and standing up against those who don't consider this aspect of communication is the responsibility of all.

Challenge Stereotypes

We discussed generational stereotypes in an earlier chapter, but here we need to discuss the other stereotypes found in the workplace. Dismiss stereotypes of people of color or different ethnic backgrounds, as well as those with varying sexual orientation or gender. You should then actively work to dismiss these stereotypes when working with other coworkers. Make sure that any time you see a stereotype being used to judge someone that you speak up and point out the ways the individual transcends those stereotypes.

Talk To Your Employer About Inclusion Programs

If your employer doesn't have a diversity and inclusion program, talk to them about implementing one. You might be surprised at the response, especially if you are willing to participate in the legwork to make it happen. This sort of initiative can also help you advance your own career even while you are championing diversity and inclusion in the workforce. If your employer already has a program in place but you feel it is inadequate, speak up and let them know how you think it can be improved.

In short, get involved, and stay involved, in your company's diversity and inclusion efforts.

12

EMBRACING REMOTE WORK AND FLEXIBILITY

W ITH MANY GEN ZERS entering the workforce during and since the pandemic, the rise of remote work and the gig economy has likely made you come to expect this element in your work structure. According to OECD Data, about 6.6% of the labor force in the United States is self-employed, freelancer, or solopreneur, all of whom make up the gig economy. However, the percentage of Gen Z identifying as self-employed or freelance is 7 percent (Statista, 2023).

Meanwhile, Forbes reports that among those aged 24 to 35, which includes both Gen Z and Millennials, 39% work remotely full-time, and another 25% work remotely at least part of the time (Haan, 2023). They also reported that 99% of respondents surveyed by Indeed said that they would like the option to work remotely at least part of the time.

In short, you're not alone in wanting to work remotely, and more jobs can be part-time remote than you might think. Some of the most common jobs that are done remotely include:

Accounting

Administrative Assistance

Computers

Customer Service

Finance

Graphic Design

Human Resources

Information Technology

Marketing

Project Management

Recruiting

Wellness

Writing

Unless you have a retail, public-facing, or service job, you can probably work remotely in a pinch, even if it is just for the purpose of avoiding sick days. You need to decide now how important working remotely is to you. There are many reasons a traditional work structure might not work for you.

Quality of Life/Work Balance: As mentioned earlier, as a generation you tend to prioritize life over work. While this can be seen as a negative trait in the traditional workplace, the remote workplace gives you more flexibility to live in the way you wish while still keeping an employer happy.

Avoiding Burnout: You were likely raised by Generation X or Millennials who struggle in their careers and get burned out in jobs because they work insane hours. It is natural that you wouldn't want to follow in their footsteps. When you are working remotely with a flexible schedule, you can prioritize life and avoid burnout. It is also easier to turn down overtime if you are not in an office setting.

However, beware that new studies are showing that there could be a correlation between increased burnout and workers who are 100% remote. It is hard to separate work from life when they occur in the same place all the time. Hybrid remote workers are the most well-balanced.

Working Remotely Increases Productivity: While it doesn't work for everyone, working remotely could increase productivity so that you can improve job performance while working fewer hours. Forbes reports that several companies have conducted in-house studies by randomly assigning workers to remote, hybrid, or in-office work. These studies are showing significant improvements in productivity and job performance, as well as resulting in fewer sick days (Tsipursky, 2022).

Working With Others 40 Hours Per Week Is Unnecessary: Teamwork is an important part of productivity and efficiency in some careers, but working within teams all the time is both unnecessary and stressful for employees. A study of several companies revealed that while productivity and financial gains increased for the company, working in teams all the time resulted in more stress for the employees, leading to greater and faster burnout (Ogbonnaya, 2019). A hybrid scenario in which one works within a team part of the time and independently the rest of the time is ideal for both organizations and you, the employee.

These things have become more apparent since the pandemic. According to Statista, 47% of surveyed workers never worked remotely before the pandemic, but 45% of workers were working remotely five or more days per week by the end of 2020 (Statista, 2023). A total of 64% of workers will be remote part or full-time in 2023. This clearly shows that remote work is the new norm and here to stay. You may never know a fully traditional workplace.

And you are best poised to thrive in this new landscape. Generation Z are digital natives, living on a screen. That makes you more likely to thrive in the remote workplace. For example, 21% of digital nomads are Generation Z, with another 37% younger Millennials (Pofeldt, 2023). This is because you don't feel tied down to the traditional workplace and your generation is more likely to disrupt the status quo.

On the downside, Generation Z needs frequent face-to-face feedback that isn't available in a fully remote position. As such, the best work environment for most Generation Z is a hybrid remote work environment, where you go into the office for meetings and teamwork but work remotely part-time.

Creating a work structure that's right for you requires taking control of your own career and understanding what that entails. Understanding your own needs is the first step in creating a work structure that works for you. Without understanding what makes you productive and efficient, you will be unable to determine if remote work is right for your work style.

From there, you have three options to incorporate remote work into your structure:

Be selective about where you work. Only apply for positions in companies that are already allowing remote work. By doing this you will decrease the number of opportunities for which you will apply, but you are also ensuring that you will have that element in your work structure. Only do this if remote work is of high importance to you.

Negotiate remote work into your contracts. Whether you are working as an employee or a freelancer, build remote work into your contracts. By having the option for remote work at least part-time in your contract, you are ensured that you can't be fired for working remotely when you find it necessary.

Design a more self-driven career. If you want to work 100% remotely, build your own schedule, and answer to none but yourself, a self-driven career through freelancing or self-employment might be the way to go. You can still use the tools learned in this book to win clients if that is the route you decide to go. Meanwhile, platforms like Upwork and Fiverr make it easy to get started in gig work of just about any kind. They offer training and payment protection, but it comes at a cost. Take this route if you're certain you can't be successful in a traditional workplace.

End of Chapter Exercise

In this exercise, you will explore your ideal work structure.

Exercise 1

Describe your ideal working environment. Consider what will help you remain focused on your work and efficient.

_____

_____

_____

_____

_____

Exercise 2

Describe your ideal workday routine. Consider what makes you the most productive and ensures accuracy.

_____

_____

_____

_____

_____

Exercise 3

Brainstorm steps you can take to integrate these needs into your real work structures and routines.

_____

_____

_____

_____

_____

13

THE SUSTAINABLE WORKPLACE

G ENERATION Z IS THE most environmental generation to date. According to Pew Research, 67% of Generation Z and 71% of Millennials believe that ensuring a sustainable planet is important for future generations (Tyson, 2021). Yet the same report states that only 32% of Generation Z have personally taken action to improve the environment.

This could stem from the fact that, other than reducing the amount of consumables purchased and purchasing from sustainable companies, Generation Z doesn't really know how to make environmental changes on a personal or organizational level. According to reporting by Forbes, Deloitte recently found that 45% of Generation Z have stopped buying brands because they are sustainable, and 50% of Generation Z have reduced what they buy (Paoletti, 2022). The same article points out that the other major way Generation Z inspires environmental change is through social media.

What you may not realize is that you have the opportunity to drive environmental change at work as well. You can instill and inspire sustainability in the workplace in a number of ways. Just speaking out about what you believe in is a great way to start, but there are more actionable things you can do to create a sustainable workplace, even if you are not responsible for ordering or packaging design.

Driving sustainability within manufacturing companies is a much clearer path than sustainability in an office or corporate setting. In manufacturing, you can make suggestions for more sustainable methods and packaging. But in a corporate or office setting, your contributions might need to be just as direct.

Here are some ways you can create a sustainable workplace regardless of the industry and company you work for.

Make the Hybrid Remote Work Structure the New Norm

You can make your hybrid remote work structure the new norm by pushing for it in your contracts and encouraging others in your workplace to do the same. A hybrid remote work structure reduces the number and frequency of vehicles on the roads, reducing each individual's carbon footprint. In addition, the company will be able to use less energy, water, and other resources with fewer staff on premises at any given time.

The best way to foster a hybrid remote work environment is to talk about its benefits to your coworkers and managers. You will see immediately that others are willing to try this new form of working to save gas and the environment, as well as having more control over their work/life balance.

Start a Carpooling Program

You don't necessarily need your employer's cooperation to start a carpooling program. Carpooling can be a very informal endeavor in which you simply talk to other people in your department with your schedule and work out a way for everyone to get to work on time with fewer cars on the road.

Once your carpooling efforts are recognized by colleagues and managers, you will be surprised at how quickly it catches on. The price of gas continues to be in flux, and it is a source of contention for many people. Carpooling reduces those costs, even if that individual is not concerned about the environment.

Offer Suggestions on Procedures to Reduce Paper

Speaking up during project meetings and while learning on the job shows initiative, so don't be afraid to do so. If you see the opportunity to save paper or other resources, speak up and let your bosses know. You might be able to institute some new policies, streamline some processes, and save some paper and energy in the process.

You should also consider starting a recycling program. It can start as simple as bringing in a bucket to recycle your own paper. Make sure you're not violating any company policies by taking that paper out of the office. Barring this caveat, you should be able to recycle most of the paper that you use in the office. When others mention it, and they will, you can offer to take their paper to the recycling center along with your own. The trend could grow from there to a company-wide movement.

Start a Recycling Program

Starting an official recycling program may require certain procedures through your managers, but in many cases, you can start recycling on your own. It starts with paper as mentioned above, but it doesn't have to end there. You can bring in a bin to recycle aluminum cans, and take it to the recycling center yourself.

Another option might be to recycle plastic. You can bring in a separate bin for plastic, if your workplace allows, or you can sort the recycling on your own after the fact. It's true that this requires some time and effort on your part, but it won't be long before others in the office are ready to help. With enough participation, you could force the company's hand to implement a true recycling program.

Get Your Work Community Involved

There are always opportunities in the community to bring awareness to or alleviate poverty, social issues, homelessness, and environmental hazards. Getting your work community involved in your local community is one way that you can drive a sustainable workplace.

This is easier than you might think. Develop sign-up sheets and circulate them around the office. You will be surprised at how many people are willing to help with various initiatives or attend community awareness events. Even if your coworkers are looking at these opportunities as social events, you will be raising their awareness as well.

Most workplaces don't interfere when employees make plans with one another but make sure that you make it clear that it isn't a company-sponsored event to avoid complications.

Request Green Office Supplies

Using recycled paper and office supplies made sustainably is a great way to drive sustainability in the workplace. Most offices will allow a budget for the office supplies their workers request to perform their jobs, as long as those costs are within reason. As you tout the praises of green office supplies and add your own to the order, you'll find that more people in the office do the same.

Look for opportunities to request the use of green materials in the course of business. You'll be surprised at how many there are. Speak up when you see these opportunities, but not necessarily in the moment. Make sure that you have a plan for switching to greener materials that are attractive to the company, such as a supplier that will save costs over less environmentally-conscious supplies.

Put Forward Sustainable Vendors on Projects

As a Gen Zer, you're likely to be in an entry-level position, or close to it. As such, you will find yourself with tasks that no one else on the team wants to perform, such as finding and arranging vendors. If you are part of a project task force, and this is part of your job, you should be using this to your advantage in furthering a sustainable workplace.

Unless vendors must be approved by your supervisors, choose vendors that you know to be sustainable companies. If vendors must be approved by your manager, bring them a few more sustainable options that you have found with similar or lower budgets. Rather than simply stating that you need to hire sustainable vendors, do the research and be prepared to state your case.

Driving Environmental Change in the Workplace

It is important to remember throughout these efforts that a company is generally interested in its bottom line above all else. You can use this fact to your advantage if you do some smart research and fast-talking.

Any time you want to start a new sustainable initiative, you should arm yourself with data. Know how the sustainable alternative will affect the bottom line, as well as how it might affect customer relationships in a positive way. You should be prepared to face any arguments with data and research to show that you have done the work, and all they must do is sign off on it.

This is the easiest way to drive environmental change in the workplace. Having a sustainable workplace and helping your company be more environmentally conscious requires diplomacy and capitalistic thinking.

PART 5: ENTREPRENEURSHIP, INNOVATION, AND STANDING ALONE

A new study by Zen Business surveyed 1,000 Generation Zers and discovered that 93% of respondents had taken a step toward investigating business ownership, and 75% ultimately want to become entrepreneurs, even if they are in a traditional career at this time (Croll, 2023). Although business ownership isn't for everyone, this entrepreneurial spirit of your generation can be put to many uses.

Let's explore the ways that you can nurture this entrepreneurial spirit to be innovative and stand alone, whether that is as a business owner, a gig worker, or an employee.

14

THE ENTREPRENEURIAL SPIRIT

O NE THING THAT YOU must not lose during your immersion into the workforce is your entrepreneurial spirit. Your generation has this entrepreneurial drive that should be nurtured regardless of your work structure or environment.

Chances are you have already dipped your hand into entrepreneurship. According to Forbes, 56% of students in 2022 said they were considering starting a new business within the next year (Drenik, 2022). Meanwhile, 43% of Gen Zers are already freelancers, which is a form of entrepreneurship (Statista, 2023). Although not all of these businesses are full-time, they do show that Generation Z is not afraid to take risks and stand on their own two feet.

While your entrepreneurial efforts may not have met with fruition as of yet, that doesn't mean you can't continue to nurture that entrepreneurial drive. As a digital native not afraid to disrupt the status quo, you are in a unique position to be a trailblazer in your chosen career field. You are hardwired to think outside the box and take risks, and this makes you very special.

Being a digital native and comfortable with technology, social media, digital communications, and e-commerce makes it easier for you to see and take advantage of entrepreneurial opportunities. Being unafraid to disrupt the status quo means that you are poised to solve the world's problems in unique ways previously thought impossible. And, because you are likely used to figuring things out on your own, you don't feel the need for someone to hold your hand while you solve those problems.

There are many ways you can foster this entrepreneurial spirit throughout your career. Here are some examples of how you can be an entrepreneur even while you are building your career within an organization.

Never Lose Your Faith in Your Ability to Achieve

You have an innate ability to achieve great things. Your drive and spirit will help cultivate belief in yourself and of what you are capable. It is possible that in the course of taking internships and entry-level positions you could have that belief shaken. It is important not to let this happen.

The best way to ensure that you retain your entrepreneurial spirit is to work within organizations that value that spirit. At the same time, there is no rule that you can't be entrepreneurial while working a full-time job. In fact, according to Bank Rate, 53% of Gen Zers have a side hustle (Gillespie, 2023). You should be one of those Zoomers.

Retain a Growth Mindset

It is important that you have a clear vision and goals for your personal and career growth, whether or not business ownership is the ultimate goal. But having a growth mindset isn't limited to personal growth. Rather, you should be considering the growth of humanity and society as a whole. This broad forward thinking will foster creativity and give you many ideas for furthering your vision and goals for yourself and the world.

Be Prepared to Stand Alone

While workplaces are often designed to take advantage of teamwork, it is still important to stand alone. You must be able to work independently and come up with new ideas without input from others. You should be able to cultivate those ideas, do the required research, and bring those ideas to fruition.

All of this requires some specific soft and technical skills. You need to be able to handle time management and project management, as well as have a strong work ethic and attention to detail. All of these qualities are those sought by employers, so there is no reason you shouldn't cultivate these traits to maintain an entrepreneurial spirit in anything that you do.

Never Stop Networking

Networking isn't just something you do when you are looking for a job. You need to be networking within your industry, career field, and age group frequently and productively. Attend at least one networking event per week if possible, even if it is simply within your own place of work. You should also strive to take advantage of mentorship opportunities, both as mentor and mentee.

Networking is a big part of entrepreneurship. You never know where you might find your next business partner.

Be Ready to Take Action

It doesn't do you much good to be forward-thinking if you don't take action. When you have an entrepreneurial idea, run with it. The worst thing you can do is fail, and every failure is a lesson that can be applied to future endeavors. The best way to learn how to be an entrepreneur is to just do it. You can get assistance and feedback from bosses and mentors, but in the end the best experience is hands-on experience. You never know what might be successful, and all of your entrepreneurial experiences will be beneficial in some way.

Practice Innovation

Innovation takes practice and resilience. How do you practice innovation? Tackle problems as soon as they arise, no matter how big or small. Make an effort to find a better way to do that project or a better method to perform that task. Even if you are not able to come up with wonderfully new ideas every time, the practice will allow you to come up with stellar ideas for start-ups and new technology that could eventually make a big impact.

Remain Competitive

You may have realized by now that the workforce is a very competitive place, and the entrepreneurial world is as well. You may be a stranger to competition up to this point, but you won't be able to say that for long. Competition is an important driving force among Generation Z of which you may not yet be self-aware.

A competitive nature breeds creativity, resilience, and out-of-the-box thinking. When you consider that you are competing against other professionals of a similar background, you will quickly realize that you must stand apart in some way. How you are unique and what you have to offer the world varies by individual, but that doesn't mean you can't embrace competitiveness in your career to foster that entrepreneurial spirit.

Continue to Take Risks

One of the things that makes Generation Z magical is that you are not afraid to take risks. You must keep that attitude if you want to nurture your entrepreneurial spirit. The risks don't have to be big, and they don't have to be financial. Taking risks simply means that you are willing to try something new, make mistakes, and learn from them for the next venture.

15

INTRAPRENEURSHIP

E ntrepreneurship isn't for everyone. Owning a business or founding a start-up requires much more than great ideas and an entrepreneurial spirit. Thankfully, you don't need to found a start-up to be an entrepreneur. Intrapreneurship is how you take that entrepreneurial spirit into the workforce.

And this intrapreneurship is both anticipated and facilitated by companies. Every business journal and magazine has run an article about the innovation of Generation Z. Your digital prowess, creative forward out-of-the-box thinking, willingness to take risks, and adaptability make your generation prime innovators.

Companies know this, and they encourage it. At Amazon, any employee of any level can put forward new ideas, and they are rewarded for doing so. Alexa and Amazon Prime memberships both came from this process. Google has a Founders Program that offers stock in exchange for profitable innovation. Tesla has a similar program. Other companies that notably foster and expect innovation from Gen Zers include Apple, Samsung, Salesforce, and Proctor & Gamble.

There are many ways you can grow your intrapreneurial spirit, but it starts with working in organizations that value your input and make it easy to innovate at any level. Consider what work environment would inspire innovation in your daily practices, and look for organizations that offer that culture.

Here are some other ways you can keep your entrepreneurial spirit while working within established organizations.

Look for Opportunities for Intergenerational Collaboration

In one study, 63% of Gen Zers felt it was important to collaborate with coworkers of varying age groups and experience levels (EY, 2018). In another study of teamwork mentioned earlier, collaboration among different generations has been found to be profitable and productive as well (Ogbonnaya, 2019). These studies show that companies and your generation are on the same page when it comes to intergenerational collaboration.

However, it is up to you to take advantage of these opportunities. Look for ways to work with team members of varying generations to create better outcomes for yourself, your team, and the organization. Such efforts are generally rewarded.

Embrace Failure as a Learning Experience

It is important to remember that every failure comes with a lesson to be learned. Your generation understands this and isn't afraid of failure. The study mentioned above also found that 80% of Generation Z think that embracing failure on a project makes them more innovative (EY, 2018). It is through our mistakes that we grow, in any area of life and at any age. Embracing failure has proven to be the best way to inspire innovation. Being unafraid of failure makes you more likely to take risks, and such risks are a necessity for innovation. You can't develop something new if you're afraid of it.

Look for the lessons in every failure. Sit down at the end of the day and write out anything that you might have done differently and why. Go back over it a few days later and add any fresh thoughts that you have. The next time you have a similar project, look back at those reflections and use the lessons to avoid the same mistakes the next time.

Continuously Learn New Skills and Talents

It has been mentioned before, but it stands to be reiterated that learning new skills and talents is a vital part of career growth. It is also the best way to keep innovating. Don't wait for your employer to teach you about new technology and tools that could help you innovate. Instead, watch technology news sources like CNet.com to stay up to date on the latest tools and tech in your field. Get your hands on it when you can, and take a class when you need to delve deeper.

Find Purpose in Your Organization

You might think that your purpose is outlined by your company's job description, but that is not the case. You should consider two forms of purpose in employment. The first purpose of any position is to further your career. The second purpose should be something that benefits the organization through innovation.

Go into every position with certain goals in mind. What do you want to gain from this position? What do you want to accomplish? Lay out how you can achieve those goals, make a plan, and follow it throughout your employment. Revisit the plan at least once a year to make sure that it is still realistic and that you are on track.

Remain Competitive by Taking on the Identity of the Company

Working within an organization makes you part of the team. When you take on the identity of the company during work, it makes you more invested in the organization and your impact upon it through the course of your workday. This in turn will inspire you to innovate for the company and achieve the unachievable.

Because while your generation is diverse and accepting, you're also no stranger to competition. Unlike Millennials, you have been competing your entire life. And you will continue the need to compete throughout your career, whatever that may be. That competition in and of itself inspires innovation.

Find Ways to Foster Creativity in the Workplace

There have been many studies that try to discover what best fosters creativity, but the results are generally the same. Music, meditation, and even gaming are on the list of the most common ways to foster creativity among Generation Z and Millennials. While these may not be possible in the workplace, there are other ways you can inspire creativity among yourself and your teammates.

Brainstorm a list of things that make you feel creative, then circle anything that you could take with you to the traditional workplace. Mark any items that you could incorporate into your home office with a star, assuming you have a remote or hybrid remote work structure as recommended.

Consider Project Management a Leadership Role

Project management is a leadership role, even if you are managing a very small project and are working alone. You will likely need to rely on the guidance or assistance of at least one other person while working on the project, and you are the leader in that instance. It is important to remember this and practice good leadership while you are in charge of a project.

How do you practice good leadership? By inspiring innovation and creativity among your teammates. You want to make everyone feel as though their contributions matter and are being used as appropriate. Don't dismiss anything out of hand, and build on the ideas of others.

Keep Track of Your Measurable Accomplishments

Keeping track of your accomplishments within each organization is a great way to inspire you to continue that intrapreneurial spirit. Keep a vision board or a digital document where you will list all of your measurable accomplishments. Any time you need to be innovative, or creative, or you just feel stuck, look back on that list to regain confidence.

Keeping track of your accomplishments is also important when you want to change positions or organizations. Having those details at your fingertips will make writing an effective resume much easier. There are many people who start to write a resume and are not able to list specific accomplishments because they didn't track them.

End of Chapter Exercise

Exercise 1

 In what ways can you innovate in the workplace? Explore this concept through a journal entry based on the suggestions in this chapter. Brainstorm what makes you creative and innovative, and how you can find or create this environment in the workplace. Use this to inform your decision on where to work.

_____

_____

_____

_____

_____

16

CONCLUSION

I F YOU TAKE NOTHING else away from this book, let it be that Generation Z as a whole is primed to be a catalyst for change in the workplace. While more of each succeeding generation has been more diverse, inclusive, and sustainable, Gen Z entering the workforce changes the balance of work dynamics. There will be more people under the age of 40 in the workforce than any other age group by 2030. And you can help shape that workforce.

Being a catalyst for change means standing up for what you believe in. It means speaking out when you see opportunities for diversity, inclusion, and sustainability. It requires you to think outside the box, and not allow older generations to hold you back. It requires intergenerational collaboration and communication, and the ability to see the forest for the trees.

In short, as a Gen Zer, it is up to you to truly change the world. Everyone expects it, and as such you have the best opportunity to effect that change. As the great Ruth Beter Ginsberg once said, "Be the change you want to see in the world."

The Future of Work

The future of work is the perfect environment for Generation Z. A glimpse into the future of work will show that the hybrid remote work structure will continue to become more desirable by both employees and companies, and your insistence upon that structure will help make it the norm.

Meanwhile, having multiple streams of income changes the world of work. The ability to be a freelancer or self-employed even while working a full-time job makes it possible for Generation Z to accomplish more in less time. In fact, even now 53% of Gen Zers have at least one side hustle in addition to their full-time or part-time job. Even 50% of Millennials have at least one side hustle. You can help make this the norm, which also decreases the likelihood of working overtime with ungrateful employers just to make ends meet.

Another way that the world has been waiting for the world of work to change is through technology. AI tools are becoming more and more prevalent, and older generations do not feel equipped to handle this new technology. It is up to you, Gen Zer, to make the most of this new world of artificial intelligence. You have more ideas as to what that entails, how it should be used, and how to protect the intellectual property of others while using AI tools.

In short, as a Gen Zer, you have the ability to help shape the future of work. Take that opportunity and responsibility with the importance that it truly has for the future of the workforce. You have the power – use it.

REFERENCES

3 in 4 Managers Find It Difficult to Work with Generation Z.
(2023, May 15). *Resume Builder.* Retrieved August 24, 2023,
from https://www.resumebuilder.com/3-in-4-managers-find-it
-difficult-to-work-with-genz/

*Change in remote work trends due to COVID-19 in the United
States in 2020.* (2023, July 7). *Statista.* Retrieved September 10,
2023, from https://www.statista.com/statistics/1122987/change
-in-remote-work-trends-after-covid-in-usa/

Charaba. (2022, August 3). Why your organization needs to invest
in employee development. *People Keep.* Retrieved September 5,
2023,   from
https://www.peoplekeep.com/blog/why-your-organization-need
s-to-invest-in-employee-development#:~:text=However%2C%2
0only%2040%25%20of%20employers,better%20attract%20and
%20retain%20employees.

Chart Book: Tracking the Post-Great Recession Economy. (2022, May
27). *Center on Budget and Policy Priorities.* Retrieved August 19,
2023, from https://www.cbpp.org/research/economy/tracking-t
he-post-great-recession-economy

Civilian labor force participation rate. (n.d.). Civilian Labor Force Participation Rate. *U.S. Bureau of Labor Sta-*

tistics. https://www.bls.gov/charts/employment-situation/civilian-labor-force-participation-rate.htm

Croll. (2023, July 16). Survey: GenZ may be the most entrepreneurial of all generations. *Yahoo! News.* Retrieved on September 11, 2023, f r o m https://finance.yahoo.com/news/survey-genz-may-be-the-most-entrepreneurial-of-all-generations-183626972.html?guccounter=1&guce_referrer=aHR0cHM6Ly93d3cuZ29vZ2xlLmNvbS88&guce_referrer_sig=AQAAAD8cKdI5rM1qTJK7orfAOVBvnfOF5VOKiCoPyi1YhO7CqHg48TaMN958R4op9uaTK-Piha16g3eSPaUgUZn0h-66s0oqNC_KVNc1L5u0Wwno08de_ATCAgyAIvN_qPFAg8Dj2f1MMjSLNnKcsQvqkeaZwq7NuKCT_pXDBajxPSLt#:~:text=New%20research%20from%20ZenBusiness%2C%20an,step%20toward%20exploring%20business%20ownership.%22

Dimock. (2019, January 17). Defining generations: Where Millennials End and Generation Z Begins. *Pew Research.* Retrieved August 19, 2023, from https://www.pewresearch.org/short-reads/2019/01/17/where-millennials-end-and-generation-z-begins/

Downs. (2019). Bridging the Gap: How the Generations Communicate. *Concordia Journal of Communication Research.* Retrieved September 4, 2023, from https://digitalcommons.csp.edu/comjournal/

Drenik. (2022, December 22). Why Gen-Z Is Our Next Wave Of Business Owners. *Forbes.* Retrieved on September 11, 2023, from https://www.forbes.com/sites/garydrenik/2022/12/22/why-gen-z-is-our-next-wave-of-business-owners/?sh=1ccd865789cd

Employee Tenure Summary. Economic Release. Bureau of Labor Statistics. Retrieved on September 5, 2023, from https://www.bls.gov/news.release/tenure.nr0.htm#:~:text=Demographic%20Characteristics%20In%20January%202022,3.9%20years%20in%20January%202020.

EY. (2018, September 18). Failure Drives Innovation, According to EY Survey on Gen Z. *Cision PR Newswire*. Retrieved Septembeer 11, 2023, from https://www.prnewswire.com/news-releases/failure-drives -innovation-according-to-ey-survey-on-gen-z-300714436.html

Fact Sheet: LGBT Workers in the Labor Market. (2022, June 1). *Center for American Progress*. Retrieved September 6, 2023, from https://www.americanprogress.org/article/fact-sheet-lgbt -workers-in-the-labor-market/

Freelance participation in the United States as of 2022, by generation. (2023, May 31). *Statista*. Retrieved on September 11, 2023, from h ttps://www.statista.com/statistics/531012/freelancers-by-age-us/

Gillespie. (2023, June 14). 1 in 4 young adult Americans want to turn their side hustle into a career. *Bank Rate*. Retrieved on September 11, 2023, from https://www.bankrate.com/personal-finance/millennial-and-gen -z-side-hustles/#:~:text=More%20than%20one%20in%20two,77)%20with%20a%20side%20hustle.

Gray. (2023, April 27). The Job Market for the Class of 2023: Key Skills/Competencies Employers Are Seeking and the Impact of Career Center Use. *National Association of Colleges and Employers*. Retrieved August 22, 2023, from https://www.naceweb.org/about-us/press/the-job-mar ket-for-the-class-of-2023-key-skills-competencies-employ ers-are-seeking-and-the-impact-of-career-center-use/

Gray. (2023, April 6). Employers Planning to Hire 9.1% More Interns for Summer 2023 Programs. *National Association of Colleges and Employers*. Retrieved August 24, 2023, from https://www.naceweb.org/about-us/press/employers-plan ning-to-hire-9-point-1-percent-more-interns-for-sum mer-2023-programs/

Guterman. (2020, February 10). When Do People Start Internships? *Chegg Internships.* Retrieved August 24, 2023, from https://www.internships.com/career-advice/search/when-do-people-start-internships

Haan. (2023, June 12). Remote Work Statistics And Trends In 2023. *Forbes Advisor.* Retrieved September 10, 2023, from https://www.forbes.com/advisor/business/remote-work-statistics/#sources_section

iCIMS Class of 2023 Report. (2023). Internet Collaborative Information Management Systems. Retrieved August 22, 2023, from https://www.icims.com/wp-content/uploads/2022/08/ClassOfReport_2023.pdf

Jones. (2022, February 17). LGBT Identification in the U.S. Ticks Up to 7.1%. *Gallup News.* Retrieved August 19, 2023, from https://news.gallup.com/poll/389792/lgbt-identification-ticks-up.aspx

Kelly. (2020, December 9). A Decade's Worth Of Workforce Changes Happened In 2020: Here Are The Lessons Learned And What You Need To Succeed In 2021. *Forbes.* Retrieved August 18, 2023, from https://www.forbes.com/sites/jackkelly/2020/12/09/a-decades-worth-of-dramatic-changes-have-been-compressed-into-2020-here-are-the-lessons-learned-and-what-you-need-to-succeed-in-2021/?sh=2911455f77e2

Labor force characteristics by race and ethnicity, 2021. (2023, January). *Bureau of Labor Statistics.* Retrieved September 6, 2023, from https://www.bls.gov/opub/reports/race-and-ethnicity/2021/home.htm

Maurer. (2018, July 12). Entry-Level-Experience Requirements Could Be Hurting Your Hiring. *Society for Human Resource Management.* Retrieved August 24, 2023 from https://www.shrm.org/resourcesandtools/hr-topics/talent-acquisition/pages/entry-level-experience-requirements-hurting-hiring.aspx

Minkin. (2023, May 17). Diversity, Equity and Inclusion in the Workplace. *Pew Research.* Retrieved September 6, 2023, from https://www.pewresearch.org/social-trends/2023/05/17/diversity-equity-and-inclusion-in-the-workplace/

Moss. (2022, July 1). The Pandemic Changed Us. Now Companies Have to Change Too. *Harvard Business Review.* Retrieved August 19, 2023, from https://hbr.org/2022/07/the-pandemic-changed-us-now-companies-have-to-change-too

Number of people 75 and older in the labor force is expected to grow 96.5 percent by 2030: The Economics Daily: U.S. Bureau of Labor Statistics. (2021, November 4). Number of People 75 and Older in the Labor Force Is Expected to Grow 96.5 Percent by 2030: The Economics Daily: U.S. Bureau of Labor Statistics. https://www.bls.gov/opub/ted/2021/number-of-people-75-and-older-in-the-labor-force-is-expected-to-grow-96-5-percent-by-2030.htm

Ogbonnaya. (2019, August 29). When Teamwork Is Good for Employees — and When It Isn't. *Harvard Business Review.* Retrieved on September 9, 2023, from https://hbr.org/2019/08/when-teamwork-is-good-for-employees-and-when-it-isnt

Paoletti. (2022, June 1). Gen Z And Environmental Issues: How To Earn Young Consumers' Trust. *Forbes.* Retrieved on September 10, 2023, f r o m https://www.forbes.com/sites/forbescommunicationscouncil/2022/06/01/gen-z-and-environmental-issues-how-to-earn-young-consumers-trust/?sh=4f97043b33ab

Percent of Employees Who Received Training by Type of Training. (n.d.) *Bureau of Labor Statistics.* Retrieved September 6, 2023, from https://www.bls.gov/news.release/sept.t01.htm

Pofeldt. (2023, August 31). Digital Nomadism Continues To Grow, Despite The "Back To The Office" Trend. *Forbes.* Retrieved on September 10, 2023, from https://www.forbes.com/sites/elainepofeldt/2023/08/31/digital-noma

dism-continues-to-grow-despite-the-back-to-the-office-trend/?sh=7ea194f5ed66

Self-employment Rate. (2022). *OECD Data.* Retrieved on September 8, 2023, from https://data.oecd.org/emp/self-employment-rate.htm#indicator-chart

Share of self-employed people in the United States as of March 2023, by age. (2023, March). *Statista.* Retrieved September 8, 2023, from https://www.statista.com/statistics/228346/people-who-are-self-employed-usa/

Sink or Swim: The 90-Day Trial Period. (2016, March 23). Sink or Swim: The 90-Day Trial Period: Survey: Most New Hires Have Less Than 90 Days to Prove Themselves. *PR Newswire.* Retrieved August 31, 2023, from https://www.prnewswire.com/news-releases/sink-or-swim-the-90-day-trial-period-300240006.html

Stahl. (2019, September 10). How Generation-Z Will Revolutionize The Workplace. *Forbes.* Retrieved August 19, 2023, from https://www.forbes.com/sites/ashleystahl/2019/09/10/how-generation-z-will-revolutionize-the-workplace/?sh=23449db14f53

Tsipursky. (2022, November 3). Workers Are Less Productive Working Remotely (At Least That's What Their Bosses Think). *Forbes.* Retrieved on September 9, 2023, from https://www.forbes.com/sites/glebtsipursky/2022/11/03/workers-are-less-productive-working-remotely-at-least-thats-what-their-bosses-think/?sh=17b1f999286a

Tyson. (2021, May 26). Gen Z, Millennials Stand Out for Climate Change Activism, Social Media Engagement With Issue. *Pew Research Center.* Retrieved on September 10, 2023, from https://www.pewresearch.org/science/2021/05/26/gen-z-millennials-stand-out-for-climate-change-activism-social-media-engagement-with-issue/

Unemployed Persons by Duration of Unemployment. (2023, August 4). *Bureau of Labor Statistics.* Retrieved August 26, 2023, from https://www.bls.gov/news.release/empsit.t12.htm

Witte. (2022, January 3). Gen Z is not 'coddled.' They are highly collaborative, self-reliant, and pragmatic, according to new Stanford-affiliated research. *Stanford News.* Retrieved August 19, 2023, from https://news.stanford.edu/2022/01/03/know-gen-z/

Women in the Workforce: A Databook. (2022, March). *Bureau of Labor Statistics.* Retrieved September 6, 2023, from https://www.bls.gov/opub/reports/womens-databook/2021/home.htm#:~:text=Women's%20labor%20force%20participation%20rate,per centage%20points%20to%2067.7%20percent.

Nicky Foster is a wife, mother, and writer living in Kansas City. Her diverse background in content marketing, freelance journalism, resume writing, office management, retail management, and call center management give her unique insights into the world of work.

For more than 30 years, Nicky has helped countless new graduates and adults find their place in the workforce through effective resumes and career counseling. As a manager, Nicky spent her time studying the latest management strategies designed for younger generations. Now, after 17 years in content marketing, Nicky has focused her creative efforts on publishing longer works and imparting those lessons to the masses.

Recent publications include "You Just Weren't There" in the chapbook *Nostalgia*, and "Glimpse of Poverty" in the chapbook *The Human Experience*. Nicky also writes fiction, short stories, and creative nonfiction.

Future-Proof: Motivating, Mentoring, and Maximizing the Next Generation of Changemakers

Reviews are incredibly important for independent publishers. They help us continue sharing books that resonate with readers like you. Thank you for being a part of our journey.

— *Ainslie Street Publishing*

To leave a review, simply scan the QR code with your phone's camera app. This will take you directly to Amazon's review page.